AF814787

STUDIES IN HISTORY ECONOMICS AND PUBLIC LAW

EDITED BY
THE FACULTY OF POLITICAL SCIENCE
OF COLUMBIA UNIVERSITY

VOLUME ONE HUNDRED AND SIX

CONTENTS

2

LEGISLATIVE HISTORY OF AMERICA'S ECONOMIC POLICY TOWARD THE PHILIPPINES

STUDIES IN HISTORY, ECONOMICS AND PUBLIC LAW

EDITED BY THE FACULTY OF POLITICAL SCIENCE
OF COLUMBIA UNIVERSITY

Volume CVI] [Number 2

Whole Number 240

LEGISLATIVE HISTORY OF AMERICA'S ECONOMIC POLICY TOWARD THE PHILIPPINES

BY

JOSE S. REYES

AMS Press, Inc.

New York

1967

AMS Press, Inc.
New York, N.Y. 10003
1967

Manufactured in the United States of America

PREFACE

In many respects, it is desirable to determine, at the outset, the metes and bounds of a subject for study. In this monograph on the "Legislative History of America's Economic Policy toward the Philippines" there is no attempt to follow out the results of the various phases of economic legislation. A logical and distinct dividing line may be made between the reasons that move legislators in the formulation of policies and the consequences of such legislative decisions. An examination of what Congressmen said and thus, presumably, of what they thought at the time of the passage of a particular law may or may not be of value. Insofar, however, as such an examination throws light on the Congressional mind, if such a term may be used to denote the blending of individual thoughts in an assembly, to that extent will the results be of significance in charting the course which Congress has pursued in the past and will probably pursue in the future.

The writer wishes to acknowledge his deep obligation to Professor Howard Lee McBain under whose direction and guidance this work was undertaken. Likewise is he indebted to Professor Lindsay Rogers, Professor Henry Parker Willis, and Professor Thomas Reed Powell for reading portions of the manuscript and valuable suggestions and criticism.

CONTENTS

CHAPTER I

INTRODUCTION

THE WAR WITH SPAIN

IN 1898 the people of the United States entered into war against Spain for the liberation of Cuba. The country went into the conflict in a spirit of collective exaltation that was perhaps only equalled by the later crusade to "make the world safe for democracy." As an unexpected result of the war, America came into possession of the Philippine Archipelago. The same reservoir out of which had flowed the moral indignation for the freedom of Cuba furnished the source for the missionary fervor for the redemption of the Philippines. In Cuba, the United States remembered her youth, her impulsive idealism, her unsophisticated optimism and her unclouded confidence in the future,—and Cuba became free. Ten thousand miles away to the West, in the waters of the Pacific it was no longer the young, hopeful Democracy that had dealings with a Malayan people but a World Power still as idealistic as her other self in the Pearl of the Antilles but more deeply conscious of her responsibility to other Powers, her moral trusteeship, her obligations to civilize; surveying things not with the roseate optimism of former years but with the cold realism of a mature mind. And so the Philippine Islands were retained for a course in government.

LEGISLATIVE HISTORY OF AMERICA'S ECONOMIC POLICY —THE SUBJECT

Nearly a quarter of a century has elapsed since those days. A study of particular phases of Philippine-American relationships within that period should not be without interest. In an age preeminently economic, when the stakes of diplomacy are no longer political frontiers but coal and iron deposits and world markets, when statecraft has become so intertwined with petroleum deposits as to render completely obsolete that worn-out adage of pouring oil on troubled waters, the most interesting as well as the most vital aspect of the relationship between America and the Philippines should be the economic one. What has been America's economic policy toward the Philippines?

The inquiry gains added interest when the portent and significance of the Washington Conference of 1922 are called to mind. Public attention and major policies have been gripped as never before by the glamour of the East. Even if the Orient should not prove to be the magnet that it is thought to be, the fact that it may conceivably, as some shrewd commentators observed, represent a half-way station in the journey from Washington to Geneva or a port of call in the discovery of the Old World, would of itself lend some color of justification to an examination of the economic policy toward America's Far Eastern Island possessions of the policy-making branch of the American government, that is to say, the Congress.

Policy may be gleaned, partly, from an examination of the provisions of statutes. It can be most surely and significantly found in the utterances of legislators themselves. Even if the actual should differ from the expected results of a law, the mistake in no way changes the intent and nature of the policy. Expressed in other words, the best indications of policy are to be found in the statements of lawmakers, themselves, as to what they thought when passing a certain law.

It should not be forgotten, however, that allowances ought always to be made for the proverbial grain of salt in a politician's pronouncements. Parliaments are notoriously places for words, words, words. The practice has almost hardened into precedent of indulging in rhetorical flights and unlimited idealism. It is only natural. Everyone is engaged in a general uplift movement which is termed the civilizing process. This has tended to induce the average mind to believe that the human soul finds satisfaction in contemplating the delights of musing around the airy heights of altruism and unselfishness. If such be the case with the average mind, it can not be otherwise with the average Congressman.

CHAPTER II

The Ratification of the Treaty of Paris

THE VOTE ON THE TREATY

On February 6, 1899 at twenty-five minutes after three o'clock in the afternoon, the Senate of the United States, by a vote of 57 to 27, or with a margin of only a single vote, consented to the ratification of the Treaty of Paris ending the Spanish-America war.[1] In spite of a severe snowstorm the galleries were packed with throngs anxious to be the first to receive tidings of the result. But two days previously, when America's decision still hung in the balance, the guns had spoken at Manila. The opening of hostilities marked the commencement of the effort to unwind the involved tangle of Filipino-American relations through the direct method of an appeal to arms. The American people, speaking through the affirmative votes of fifty-seven Senators, accepted, with all its unforeseeable consequences, the only controversial part of the treaty—the one involving the cession of the Philippines to the United States.[2] The reasons that swayed those fifty-seven affirmative votes will be the subject of inquiry in this chapter.

The American system of government by political parties had an inevitable effect on the fortunes of the peace treaty.

[1] For a record of the votes, see *Senate Journal*, 55th Cong., 3rd Sess., p. 216.

[2] Article III of the Treaty, 30 *Stat. L.*, p. 1754.

The bulk of the leadership of the Democratic party was opposed to the annexation of the Philippines. That annexation was not, however, the sole problem presented by the issue of whether or not the treaty should be ratified. While the Democratic Senators were still undecided as to the course they would pursue, the acknowledged leader of the party, Mr. Bryan, came to Washington and advised ratification on the ground that approval of the treaty did not necessarily mean the adoption of what the Democrats later termed as the policy of imperialism. It is impossible to ascertain just how many votes were determined by this appeal of Mr. Bryan. That it exercised an unmistakably strong influence on the doubtful Senators is asserted in no uncertain terms by Senator Hoar, one of the leaders in the anti-treaty fight.[1]

But disregarding the question of whether or not Mr. Bryan's intervention was productive of baneful or beneficial results, we turn to another side of the picture—the views of Mr. McKinley as head of the Administration and leader of the Republican party.

PRESIDENT MCKINLEY AND THE PHILIPPINES

Inasmuch as the Administration is always charged with the conduct of foreign relations and gives tone and direction to a country's foreign policy, an examination of the gradual formulation of executive policy in respect to a question relating to foreign relations is quite as indispensable as an investigation of senatorial speeches and comments.

[1] On the subject of Mr. Bryan's intervention, see Hoar, *Autobiography of Seventy Years* (New York, 1903), vol. ii, pp. 322-323; C. B. Elliot, *The Philippines to the End of the Military Regime* (Indianapolis, 1916), pp. 377-378; C. S. Olcott, *Life of William McKinley* (New York, 1916), vol. ii, p. 139; Latané, *America as a World Power* (New York, 1907), p. 77. Altogether 10 Democratic Senators voted for the treaty.

It is for this reason that the evolution of President McKinley's views on the Philippines, after the subject acquired the character of an insistent problem, is of importance in revealing that cross-section of the American mind which, on the 6th of February, 1899, accepted sovereignty over the Philippine Archipelago.

The question was brought to a head by the initiation of armistice negotiations during the last few days of July, 1898. On the 27th of that month, the newspapers published the news that Spain had sued for peace and the *New York Times,* under the heading "Problems for the President," said, in part:

> The Administration is not over-enthusiastic about keeping the Philippines, but it is known at the White House that the country has settled down to a notion that the islands are ours, and will remain so after the war is over. . . .

The following day, the *Times,* while reporting that the Administration was discouraging the idea of the retention of the entire Philippine group, stated the leaning of "Administration sources" to be toward the acquisition of a coaling station and the return of the islands to Spain with guarantees for the native inhabitants.[1] On July 29, the same paper declared the Philippine question to be "still in doubt" and the next day asserted that the President was still undecided and that differences of opinion existed in the cabinet.

Evidence of such indecision on the part of the President can also be found in the note sent by the Secretary of State to the Spanish government on the 30th of July, 1898, outlining the terms of peace acceptable to the United States. The third point in these demands provided for the occupa-

[1] *New York Times,* July 28, 1898.

tion of Manila by the United States "pending the conclusion of a treaty of peace which shall determine the control, disposition, and government" of the Philippines.[1] By Article III of the peace protocol signed at Washington on August 12, 1898, the "control, disposition, and government" of the Philippine Islands were left open for future negotiation.[2]

In the meantime, various agencies of the government were active in procuring information about the Philippines and making it available to the heads of the Executive Departments. As early as May 1898, the government geologist, Dr. George F. Becker, was sent with the first expeditionary force to the Philippines to report on the geological and mineral resources of the islands. He made his report from Manila on September 15, 1898 and on the 29th of the following October, the Secretary of the Interior transmitted this Becker report to the Secretary of State who, on the 4th of November, sent it to the American Peace Commission at Paris.[3]

A little over a month previous to the Becker report and three days before the signing of the protocol, the acting Chief Intelligence Officer of the Navy Department, Ensign Everett Hayden, had similarly prepared a memorandum for the President, pursuant to an order of the Navy Department dated the day before, on the "mineral and other resources and availability as naval stations" of the different islands of the Philippine group, and his conclusion on one point was that, strategically, the Philippine Islands were "one and inseparable."[4]

[1] *Papers relating to Foreign Relations, etc.*, pp. 820-821 published as *House Document 1*, 55th Cong., 3rd Sess.

[2] *Ibid.*, p. 828.

[3] *S. Doc.* 62, pt. i, pp. 513-518, 55th Cong., 3rd Sess.

[4] *Ibid.*, pp. 519-523.

On August 13, the day after the cessation of hostilities, the Navy Department sent the following cablegram to Dewey:

The President desires to receive from you any important information you may have of the Philippines, the desirability of the several islands, the character of their population, coal and other mineral deposits, their harbor and commercial advantages, and, in a naval and commercial sense, which would be the most advantageous. . . . [1]

Then followed a further inquiry later as to the Admiral's views on the general question of the Philippines.[2] To these two inquiries, Admiral Dewey replied on August 29, 1898. He thought the most important islands of the group were Luzon, Panay, Cebu, Negros, Leyte, and Mindanao. The first was, in his opinion, the most desirable and "therefore the one to retain." It contained Manila, the most important and populous port of the Archipelago and one that, in America's hands could "soon become one of the first ports of the world." It produced large quantities of tobacco, had cheap labor, was peopled by a gentle and docile race, was the farthest north of the big islands and, consequently, had the most temperate climate. It was "nearest the trade routes from the United State and Honolulu" to the centers of trade in the East. It commanded San Bernardino Straits, the main East-West water route through the Philippines. It, also, had Subig Bay, the "best harbor" in the islands and one which had no "equal as a coaling station or naval and military base." Therefore, the Admiral concluded that "from all the above facts" it semed patent that Luzon was "by far the most valuable

[1] *Navy Department Report*, 1898, Appendix to Navigation Bureau Report, pp. 122-123.

[2] Telegram of Mr. Hay to Mr. Day, Oct. 5, 1898, *House Document 1*, 55th Cong., 3rd Sess., p. 917.

island in the group, whether considered from a commercial or military standpoint." [1] From the best available material it was the impression of the Admiral that the islands contained varied and valuable mineral resources and admirable timber.

Turning to the official correspondence between President McKinley, through the Secretary of State, and the American Peace Commission at Paris, there is found, first, the President's letter of instructions on September 16, 1898, demanding as one of the terms of peace the cession of the island of Luzon.[2] Those instructions began with a restatement of the high moral aims that America had in entering the war. The President wished that the same "high rule of conduct" should be followed in the making of peace. The aim was to be lasting results and "the achievement of the common good under the demands of civilization," rather than ambitious designs. In the interests of permanent peace it was imperative that Spain should abandon the Western Hemisphere.

Coming to the subject of the Philippines, the instructions recognized that they stood upon a different basis from the Spanish West Indies. There had been no thought originally, the instructions further avowed, of acquisition, either complete or partial. But the victory of American arms at Manila imposed obligations that the United States could not disregard. "The march of events," the instructions said, "rules and overrules human action . . . . the war has brought us new duties and responsibilities which we must meet and discharge as becomes a great nation on whose growth and career from the beginning the Ruler of Nations has plainly written the high command and pledge of civilization."

[1] *S. Doc. 62*, 55th Cong., 3rd Sess., pp. 383-384.

[2] *H. Doc. 1*, 55th Cong., 3rd Sess., p. 828.

Incidental to America's retention of the Philippines was the commercial opportunity which American statesmanship could not ignore. America sought the open door in the Orient and what she asked for she was willing to accord to others. The opportunity that was associated with Philippine acquisition depended " less on large territorial possessions than upon an adequate commercial basis and upon broad and equal privileges."

And the concluding part of this Philippine phase of the letter of instructions ran thus:

It is believed that in the practical application of these guiding principles the present interests of our country and the proper measure of its duty, its welfare in the future, and the consideration of its exemption from unknown perils will be found in full accord with the just, moral, and humane purpose which was invoked as our justification in accepting the war.

Because of these considerations, the United States, the President said, could not accept less than the cession of the island of Luzon. It was also desirable to acquire equal rights for American vessels and merchandise entering that portion of the Philippine Archipelago not ceded to the United States. Reciprocal rights would be granted Spain in those parts under American control.

In view of the President's instruction to demand the cession of Luzon, the American Peace Commission at Paris during the latter part of October, found itself divided on the issue of whether or not to insist on the transfer of the entire Philippine group or of Luzon alone, as originally contemplated in the instructions of September 16. On the 25th of October, the Commissioners cabled a statement of their opinions to Washington and asked for further instructions. Mr. Whitelaw Reid[1] and Senators Frye and

[1] For a reference to Mr. Reid's supposed influence on President McKinley's Philippine views, see C. B. Elliot, *The Philippines to the End of the Military Regime*, p. 365. See also R. Cortissoz, *The Life of Whitelaw Reid* (New York, 1921), vol. ii, pp. 219-227.

Davis inclined toward annexation of the whole group. Inasmuch as the instructions expressly stipulated that Luzon should be ceded, the question of remaining at all in the Philippines, they thought, could not properly come up before the American Peace Commission. But the information which they had gained at Paris led them to believe that it would be a naval, political, and commercial mistake to divide the Archipelago. They, therefore, asked for an "extension of instructions."[1] On the other hand, Senator Gray, the lone Democrat of the Commission, opposed the acquisition of the Philippines, either in whole or in part, on moral grounds as well as on grounds of policy. Midway between these two views stood the Chairman of the Commission, Mr. William R. Day, who was for the retention of Luzon only. He thought that prudence dictated caution and the acceptance of limited liabilities.[2]

Promptly upon receipt of this dispatch from the Peace Commission, the Secretary of State sent an answering telegram, on October 26, 1898, giving the President's views. The Secretary said that information received by the President since the departure of the Commission had led to the conviction that the cession of Luzon alone would not be justified on "political, commercial, or humanitarian grounds." The cession should be "of the whole archipelago or none. The latter is wholly inadmissible, and the former must therefore be required."[3] Two days after, in another cablegram to the Peace Commissioners, the President further explained his attitude. The "single consideration of duty and humanity" had influenced him in his conclusion, the President declared.[4]

[1] *H. Doc. 1*, 55th Cong., 3rd Sess., p. 932.

[2] *Ibid.*, p. 935.

[3] *H. Doc. 1*, 55th Cong., 3rd Sess., p. 938.

[4] The negotiations regarding the Philippines are outlined in C. B. Elliot, *The Philippines to the End of the Military Regime*, pp. 339-356.

From this examination of the correspondence between the State Department and the Peace Commission, it is clear that on September 16, 1898 President McKinley had decided on the acquisition of Luzon alone, and by October 26th had been convinced of the necessity for Spain's cession of the whole Philippine group, which cession he was led to require on grounds of "duty and humanity." An analysis of press reports throwing light on the President's views on the Philippines during this period in the *New York Times,* a paper not unfriendly to the administration, shows considerable hesitation on the part of the President, though there was much less indecision on the part of his official advisers.

On September 5, 1898, or a little less than a month after the cessation of hostilities, the *Times* reported that the President and his advisers were becoming convinced that the country wanted the retention of all conquered territory as compensation for the cost of the war in money, human life, and suffering.

On September 14, the same paper reported a Cabinet meeting held the previous day at which no decisions were reached. The reports pictured the President as still waiting for "public sentiment to mature," ready to compromise, and opposed to the idea of conquest, though he was believed to be in favor of retaining Luzon for a coaling station, a naval base, and an opening for a market in the Orient.

The next day, the *Times* announced a meeting of the members of the Peace Commission and affirmed a continued watchful waiting by the President of the drift of public opinion. The determination to hold Luzon, however, seemed to have been agreed upon.

On the 16th, the *Times* chronicled a session of the President with the Peace Commissioners in the morning of the previous day and a special Cabinet meeting in the afternoon.

It said that the President was aware of the drift of public opinion toward retention of the Philippines and that it was not improbable that the Commission would insist on holding the Archipelago.

On September 17, the *Times* recorded the departure of the Peace Commission and carried the news that the majority of the Commission and the Cabinet was in favor of going farther in the Philippine question than the President.

Nearly a month later, President McKinley started on his swing around the circle to feel the pulse of public opinion throughout the Middle West. It will be remembered that in his instructions to the Peace Commissioners he had, on September 16, decided on the cession of Luzon. On October 12, he delivered an address at the Omaha Exposition. He said the nation could not ignore its international responsibilities in an age of "frequent interchange and mutual dependency." He counseled mature deliberation, self-control, and the avoidance of aggression. He saw his country recognizing the hand of the Almighty in the ordeal through which it had passed.[1]

In travelling through Iowa, the next day, he enumerated the things that spelled happiness for America. Sound money, abundant revenues, and unquestioned national credit were all there but what was wanted was new markets. "As trade follows the flag," he said, "it looks very much as if we were going to have new markets." [2]

At Chicago, the President commented on the enthusiastic reception he had received in the West. He interpreted it as signifying the desire of the people to preserve and write into the treaty of peace the "just fruits" of America's achievements on land and sea. And three days afterward,

[1] *New York Times*, October 13, 1898, p. 5.

[2] *Ibid.*, October 14, 1898, p. 6.

he dwelt on the currents of destiny that flowed through the hearts of the people. He expressed confidence that the American people would not interrupt the "movements of men," planned and designed by the "Master of men." [1]

In Ohio, the President referred to America's obligation to accept the trust which civilization might impose on her in the future. And at Logansport, Indiana, he again alluded to the remaining task of writing "into honorable treaty the just fruitage of the war." [2]

The last speech came only four days before the President's instructions to the Peace Commissioners to require the cession of the entire Philippine group. Before he undertook this political pilgrimage, he had already decided on the acquisition of the island of Luzon. It seems evident both from this fact and the tenor of his speeches that the President went out among the people not so much to seek light as to build up popular support for a policy already formed. [3]

In his *Life of William McKinley*, Mr. C. S. Olcott describes the developments leading to the conclusion of peace in a way that tends to confirm this conclusion. As early as the time of the drafting of the protocol the President showed his independence of judgment by putting into its terms his own conclusions. [4] The first draft made by the State Department contained a provision for the relinquish-

[1] *New York Times*, October 16, 19, 1898.

[2] *Ibid.*, October 22, 1898.

[3] A similar opinion was expressed in an editorial of the *New York Times* for October 18, 1898. In his book, *The Philippines to the End of the Military Regime*, C. B. Elliot advances the view that the President's western trip assured him of popular support for the policy of annexation but that it was the President who formulated and decided on the policy (pp. 365-366). For the view that the Western trip decided the President's Philippine policy, see Hoar, *Autobiography of Seventy Years*, pp. 309-312.

[4] C. S. Olcott, *Life of William McKinley*, vol. ii, pp. 61-67.

ment of the Philippines, with the exception of sufficient ground for a naval station. On this point opinion in the Cabinet was divided and the provision in the protocol finally agreed upon regarding the Philippines was what the President had had in mind from the very beginning. At this time the minds of the Cabinet members were swayed by different motives. Secretary Wilson had a work of evangelization in mind, while Secretaries Bliss and Griggs were the apostles of commerce. Three other Secretaries—Messrs. Gage, Long, and Day—wanted a naval base only, although one of them, Mr. Gage, later changed his mind and became a convinced commercial expansionist.[1]

After the signing of the protocol the President endeavored to secure from the men he trusted information regarding conditions in the Philippines. Thus, in the early part of October, 1899, he had a conversation with Admiral Dewey and a copy of the President's own memorandum of this conversation is found in Mr. Olcott's book.[2] The President gathered from the Admiral that the Filipinos were not capable of self-government; that Aguinaldo had only 40,000 followers out of eight or ten million people; and that it was the duty of the United States to keep the Islands permanently. They were valuable in every way and should not be given up. There were stories of church desecration and cruelities perpetrated by the insurgent government.

It was probably out of such information which these and similar statements contained that the President ultimately came to believe that it was America's moral duty to demand the cession of the Philippines.[3]

[1] C. S. Olcott, *Life of William McKinley*, vol. ii, pp. 62-63. For the views of John Hay, who became Secretary of State later, see Thayer, *Life and Letters of John Hay* (Boston, 1915), p. 198.

[2] *Ibid.*, vol. ii, p. 97.

[3] *Ibid.*, vol. ii, pp. 109-111 gives an account of how President McKinley decided to require the cession of the Philippines.

On December 17, 1898, a week after the signing of the treaty, the President spoke at Savannah, Georgia. He stressed America's duty toward the struggling people of the Philippines, quoted a poem of Bryant's breathing confidence in America's future, and ended with a determination to keep the "covenants" which "duty" made for the United States in 1898. It was on this same occasion that Mr. Gage, the Secretary of the Treasury, in replying to the toast "commerce," hailed it as the source of profit and the pioneer of civilization, touched on the underlying law impelling advanced nations to share their blessings with backward peoples, and made the unfortunate and infelicitous reference to "philanthropy and five per cent." [1]

Four days before the ratification of the Paris peace treaty, President McKinley sent a message to the Christian Endeavor Society of Boston on the subject of expansion. "The expansion of our country," the message ran, "means the expansion of our system of education, of our principles of free Government, of additional securities to life, liberty and the pursuit of happiness, as well as of our commerce and of the distribution of the products of our industries and labor." [2]

It seems certain from these public declarations of the President that regard for America's economic and strategic interests and a vague sense of obligation to Providence and civilization were the considerations uppermost in his mind at the time of the peace negotiations in Paris. How far the conclusions in one sphere became father to the thoughts in the other is, at best, a subject for guesswork. The President in his letter of instructions of September 16, 1898 in which he directed the Commissioners to demand the cession of Luzon said:

[1] *New York Times*, December 18, 1898.

[2] *Ibid.*, February 3, 1899, p. 3.

It is believed that in the practical application of these guiding principles the present interests of our country . . . will be found in full accord with the just, moral, and humane purpose which was invoked as our justification in accepting the war.

If, it might be asked, the measure of America's duty, irrespective of present or future national interests, comprehended within its limits the acquisition of the Philippines, how was it possible that those limits excluded all the islands of the Philippine group other than Luzon? Surely the duties that civilization imposed with respect to the other islands had at least a magnitude and urgency equal to those that were faced and accepted when the retention of Luzon was decided upon on September 16, 1898.

About a month later, on October 26, the President cabled the Peace Commission to demand the cession of the entire Archipelago because information had reached him since the departure of the peace envoys which convinced him that the acquisition of Luzon, alone, could not be justified on "political, commercial, or humanitarian grounds." [1] In other words, the acquisition of Luzon having been decided upon previously, and the islands being strategically and otherwise "one and inseparable"—to quote the words of the Acting Chief Intelligence officer of the Navy Department on August 9, 1898 [2]—logic, if not the tide of circumstances, required the retention of the Philippine Islands. Two days after the President's telegram of the 26th of October, he sent another message to the Peace Commissioners wherein he avowed that the "single consideration of duty and humanity" had influenced his decision. In his letter of instructions to the Peace Commission on Sep-

[1] *Papers relating to Foreign Relations, etc.*, p. 935, published as *House Document 1*, 55th Cong., 3rd Sess. See also Senator Foraker's speech, *Congressional Record*, 57th Cong., 1st Sess., p. 5294.

[2] *S. Doc. 62*, 55th Cong., 3rd Sess., p. 521.

tember 16, 1898, the President had shown himself not unmindful of the bearing which annexation of the Philippines had on American economic interests.[1] Yet on October 26, he declared that the single consideration of duty and humanity was the only factor that had entered into his decision. Was this a case of carrying over a conclusion from the particular to the general? Did the concepts of duty toward the United States determine those toward mankind? These questions, if incapable of being answered accurately, are still interesting subjects for speculation.

THE SENATE AND THE PEACE TREATY

When the President submitted the Treaty of Paris, signed on December 10, 1898, to the Senate of the United States on January 4, 1899,[2] the only proposition that seemed likely to meet with opposition was the article relating to the cession of the Philippine Islands. Around that issue raged a fierce controversy between expansionists, sometimes termed imperialists, and the anti-imperialists. The two sides could not meet on a single, clear-cut issue. Intertwined as that issue happend to be with the question of making peace, Senators had to consider the argument in favor of ratifying the peace treaty and settling the Philippine question afterward. And the expansionists were of various hues, some frankly avowing considerations of commercial and strategic policy as the chief factors involved and others striking notes of varying metaphysical concepts. The anti-imperialists were similarly divided. A few believed thoroughly in the literal application of the principles of the Declaration of Independence; others would recognize realities to the extent of leading the Philippine people by the hand to a status more or less independent, while still others con-

[1] *Supra*, p. 18.

[2] *S. Doc. 62*, 55th Cong., 3rd Sess., p. 3.

cerned themselves primarily with the effect on America's social system of the incorporation of a vast number of Asiatics who were, racially, of doubtful standing and antecedents.

Ratification came on February 6, 1899 in the shape of 57 yea votes as against 27 votes for the nays. For the affirmative side were counted 39 Republican Senators, 10 Democrats, 3 Populists, 4 Silverites, and 1 Independent.[1] Thirty out of these fifty-seven Senators gave reasons for their vote during the course of the debate or in the succeeding sessions of Congress in the four years immediately following.

The thirty Senators who felt the inward urge strong enough to allow the public to view their mental processes may be divided into five groups, based on the nature of the reasons they gave for their affirmative votes.

THE PEACE GROUP

First, there was the group actuated by the desire to conclude peace with Spain and postpone the settlement of the Philippine problem. Two propositions formed the basis of this line of policy. One was that the interests of the United States required the conclusion of peace with Spain. And the other, sometimes regarded as a supplement to the first and at other times looked upon as of fundamental importance, asserted that ratification did not necessarily mean the acceptance of a colonial policy by the United States.

Seven Senators specifically named peace as the controlling motive of their vote for ratification, namely, Senators Allen, Clay, Gray, Kenney, Ross, Spooner, and Teller.

The Populist Senator from Nebraska, Mr. Allen, delivered a constitutional argument affirming the doctrine

[1] *N. Y. Times*, February 7, 1899. See also *Senate Journal*, 55th Cong., 3rd Sess., p. 216.

that mere seizure of territory did not mean annexation and that the provisions of the Constitution, with the exception of the right of suffrage, extended to the inhabitants of every territory and district of the United States.[1] Later, Senator Allen denied that his vote for the treaty meant a vote for annexation. "I do it," he said, "for the simple reason that in my judgment the Government of the United States cannot afford to open up negotiations with the Spanish dynasty again. We have the whole question within our jurisdiction and within our power, and here and by us alone it should be settled."[2]

Senator Clay, a Democrat from Georgia, had much the same reasons as Senator Allen. He admittted the right of the United States to acquire territory and to govern such a territory but only with a view to ultimate admission as a state. Vigorously combating the notion of acquiring the Philippines and governing them without constitutional limitations, he confessed himself appalled at the theoretical possibility of 9,000,000 Asiatics leaving their homes and settling in Georgia, New York, or any other place and acquiring rights of citizenship; he foresaw the danger of international friction in the Far East, remembered the teachings of history on the government of subject provinces by free nations, and predicted increased military and naval expenses. He was unalterably opposed to the annexation and permanent retention of the Philippines. Nevertheless, he could not vote against the treaty because those "great problems must sooner or later be settled by the action of an American Congress" and "to reject the treaty would be to make the complications more serious, the responsibilities greater;" and because the problems growing out of the

[1] *Cong. Record*, 55th Cong., 3rd Sess., pp. 573-574.

[2] *Ibid.*, pp. 1481, 1737.

war could be more satisfactorily settled the sooner peace was definitely agreed upon.[1] Three years afterwards, Senator Clay reiterated the same reasons with the added statement that at the time of ratification he did not believe that Congress would pursue the policy it had theretofore followed.[2]

The Democratic representative on the Peace Commission, Senator Gray, though another anti-expansionist, had to "choose between evils" and finally voted for peace, trusting the American people to settle the Philippine question aright.[3]

A little over a year after the vote on the treaty, Senator Kenney expressed his view that "of the influences which moved members of this Senate to vote for the treaty the most powerful were the desire to end the war and commence the work of liberty and freedom in those far-off islands. . . . To continue the war conditions, fearing unjust treatment by the United States of those who had aided us . . . . seemed unreasonable and without foundation; certainly so in the face of assurance made by those who should have been able to speak on the subject".[4]

Senator Ross of Vermont, did not see any obstacles, legal or otherwise, in the way of annexation of the Philippines and supported the peace treaty in order that peace conditions might be established.[5]

In a speech that attracted attention and exerted a powerful influence, Senator Spooner, one of the leaders on the Republican side, summarized in beautiful language the reasons which swayed his decision. He admitted frankly

[1] *Cong. Record*, 55th Cong., 3rd Sess., pp. 964-965, 1484.

[2] *Cong. Record*, 57th Cong., 1st Sess., p. 6096.

[3] *N. Y. Times*, January 15, 1899, p. 5, and January 31, 1899, p. 5.

[4] *Cong. Record*, 56th Cong., 1st Sess., p. 1968.

[5] *N. Y. Times*, Feb. 7, 1899.

that he was a commercial expansionist; yet, even from that standpoint, he was not convinced of the wisdom of retaining the Philippines. "Some gentlemen," he remarked, "waltz up to this proposition of territorial expansion as gaily as 'the troubadour touched his guitar'. I can not do it. I have not been able to persuade myself that the best interests of this country in the long run—and we ought to study its interests for the long run—are to be subserved by a policy of territorial expansion, permanent dominion over far distant lands and peoples."

Notwithstanding these doubts, he would ratify the treaty and thus bring peace to the country. He would accept sovereignty and title, do what was right, and leave the American people to decide on a permanent policy.[1]

Still another Senator who voted for bringing on a state of peace was Senator Teller of Colorado. The author of the famous resolution with respect to Cuba found his judgment influenced by reasons as conflicting as they were powerful. On December 20, 1898 the idea of a crusade for human freedom and good government and the fulfillment of America's mission governed his imagination.[2] On January 24, 1899, he wanted the treaty ratified in the interest of the Filipino people.[3] But on the first day of the following month, he delivered a speech along lines which he had not touched till then. After devoting much attention to proving the Filipinos incapable of self-government, he discoursed on the general situation in the Orient, emphasizing the need of retaining the footing which the United States had acquired through means almost providential. He talked about coal deposits in the Philippines and asserted

[1] *Cong. Record*, 55th Cong., 3rd Sess., pp. 1385, 1388.

[2] *Cong. Record*, 55th Cong., 3rd Sess., p. 327.

[3] *Ibid.*, p. 969.

that control of coal deposits meant commercial and military domination.[1] And a year later, he said:

. . . I believe myself that the interest of the United States—and I was looking after their interest and not that of the Filipinos — requires that we should ratify the treaty. I was anxious for its immediate ratification.[2]

On June 4, 1900, he again referred to the ratification of the treaty and said ratification had been necessary to prevent the consequences, injurious to America, which a continuation of the war would have entailed.[3] On January 16, 1901 he declared that he had not been in favor of giving up the Philippines, that he had believed that their retention would be better for the Filipinos and might have been very valuable to the United States, but that he had never contemplated holding them by force.[4]

Three Senators belonging to the Republican party favored ratification of the treaty and decision on the Philippine problem in due time after the ratification. Senator T. C. Platt of New York did not know and did not think anybody knew what ought to be done with the Philippines; but, this, he knew, that the islands should be withdrawn from Spanish sovereignty and their disposition placed in America's hands.[5] In a mood entirely different from the unruffled confidence which Mr. Platt displayed, Senator Wellington of Maryland voted for the treaty because of assurances which he thought he obtained from the Administration against a policy of forcible annexation and permanent

[1] *N. Y. Times*, February 2, 1899, p. 5.

[2] *Cong. Record*, 56th Cong., 1st Sess., p. 1333.

[3] *Ibid.*, p. 6510.

[4] *Cong. Record*, 56th Cong., 2nd Sess., p. 1080. See also *ibid.*, p. 535 and *Cong. Record*, 57th Cong., 1st Sess., p. 2024.

[5] *Cong. Record*, 55th Cong., 3rd Sess., p. 1155.

retention.[1] Three years after the ratification, the Maryland Senator considered those pledges to him to have been broken and said:

> . . . I would give very much, I would today give ten years of my life, to recall the vote that I gave upon the ratification of the treaty. I want to go further and say again, as I have said before, that the promises which were made to me upon that occasion were broken by the Administration, and if I could now recall my vote I would do so.[2]

Mason, of Illinois, was another Senator whose vote seemed to have been determined by promises of what was to happen in the future. He had been assured, he said, that ratification would stop the war in the Philippines.[3] His own judgment inclined against approval of the treaty. The state legislature and the people of his state were for ratification yet he "never would have voted for the treaty, if it had not been the open and notorious understanding that we were to have a vote upon a resolution on the same day, declaring our intention to give to the Philippines self-government as soon as, in the opinion of the people of the United States, they were equal to the task."[4]

Thus these three Senators voted "aye"; one because he had confidence in the future and the other two because they thought that future would disclose something which, later events proved, did not appear.

[1] *Cong. Record*, 56th Cong., 1st Sess., p. 938 also *Cong. Record*, 56th Cong., 2nd Sess., p. 534 and *Cong. Record*, 57th Cong., 1st Sess., pp. 1852-1853.

[2] *Cong. Record*, 57th Cong., 1st Sess., p. 2022.

[3] *Cong. Record*, 55th Cong., 3rd Sess., p. 1844.

[4] *Cong. Record*, 57th Cong., 1st Sess., p. 6160.

PATRIOTISM AS A MOTIVE FOR RATIFICATION

A trio of Senators, of three different political faiths, assigned patriotism, the desire to support the Administration and the flag, as the reasons for their votes for ratification. J. P. Jones, a Silverite Senator from Nevada, feared the ruin of the country as a result of the policy of expansion and would not have voted for the treaty if a vote for it meant a vote for expansion. But the hostilities in Manila had produced a crisis. He took it as a patriotic duty to vote for the treaty.[1] A somewhat complicated case was that of Senator J. L. McLaurin, a Democrat from South Carolina. In a speech on January 13, 1899, he termed himself a moderate expansionist but said he desired American expansion to be confined within the limits of North America. He believed that position to be the only one "in harmony with the Constitution and the spirit and genius of republican institutions."[2] On the day set for voting on the treaty, Senator McLaurin delivered a brief statement setting forth his reasons for giving an affirmative vote in spite of his previous stand against acquisition of the Philippines. He regarded the agreement to pass the McEnery resolution as a pledge against expansion and felt obliged to uphold the hands of the Administration in the crisis that had developed at Manila.[3] A little less than two years after ratification, Senator McLaurin again declared that he would have been found among the opponents of the treaty, if hostilities had not occurred in the Philippines.[4] Although the conflict at Manila may have in fact decided Senator McLaurin's vote, the Senator was not entirely unaware of the existence of

[1] *N. Y. Times*, Feb. 7, 1899.

[2] *Cong. Record*, 55th Cong., 3rd Sess., pp. 638-642.

[3] *N. Y. Times*, February 7, 1899.

[4] *Cong. Record*, 57th Cong., 1st Sess., p. 219.

strong reasons for the retention of the islands. On February 28, 1900 he stated his belief that the cause of "the advent of the United States in the Orient is the hand of Providence directing and guiding us to our destiny." He believed that the retention would "prove a blessing in the extension" of trade and commerce. However, it was a question not of profit and loss but of "right and national duty." Farther on, he expressed the opinion that there was a "commercial necessity for holding the Philippines," because "in the Orient the commercial possibilities exceed the wildest dreams of the optimist."[1] At the end of this speech, he inserted a copy of his answer to the plea, under date of October 12, 1899, of cotton manufacturers of his state for the open door in China. He gave it as his judgment that the acquisition of the Philippines gave to the United States "paramount political and commercial advantages" and constituted the "only safeguard" for her trade interests in that portion of the world. He believed that admission as "American citizens of millions of the semi-barbarous inhabitants of a tropical country" was not a necessary result of the commercial expansion which was desired. For the people of the Southern States, the Philippine question held momentous consequences.[2] The completeness of Senator McLaurin's recovery on February 28, 1900 from the fears entertained on January 13, 1899[3] found demonstration in these concluding sentences of his speech:

Under a destiny unforseen and uncontrollable by us, the power and institutions of the United States have been planted in the East. I believe that if we do our duty, it means not only the elevation and uplifting of the peoples of that far-off land, but

[1] *Cong. Record*, 56th Cong., 1st Sess., pp. 2382-2385.

[2] *Ibid.*, p. 2385.

[3] *Cong. Record*, 56th Cong., 3rd Sess., pp. 638-642.

that it will add to the power and glory of our free institutions, and the commercial supremacy of the nation.[1]

In the case of the third Senator, Mr. W. J. Sewell, of New Jersey, sentiment for the country and the flag appear to have been wholly responsible for his views on Philippine acquisition.[2]

EXPANSION AS A MOTIVE

Different brands of expansionism there were. One emphasized prestige, another commercial power, a third strategic considerations, and the last that inward urge disclosed in the successive waves of expansion, which had spanned the continent and was on the verge of reaching the farther shores of the Pacific.

Senator J. C. Burrows, of Michigan, in the course of a review of the achievements of President McKinley's first term, referred with evident approval to the banishment of Spanish dominion from the Western Hemisphere and the establishment of American power in the Orient, to the great advantage of America's trade in the Pacific.[3]

A different aspect of the war's results appeared upon the intellectual horizon of the Senator from Illinois, Mr. S. M. Cullom. To him, the war furnished an opportunity for the United States to assume the position of a great world power which she "could not have acquired by a century of peace."[4]

Senator C. K. Davis, of Minnesota, one of the five Commissioners who negotiated the peace treaty and who was chairman of the Senate Committee on Foreign Relations,

[1] *Cong. Record*, 56th Cong., 1st Sess., p. 2386.

[2] *Cong. Record*, 56th Cong., 1st Sess., p. 1332.

[3] *N. Y. Tribune*, June 8, 1900, p. 2. See also the *N. Y. Times*, August 4, 1898, p. 1.

[4] *Cong. Record*, 57th Cong., 1st Sess., p. 6155.

favored expansion for strategic and commercial reasons. As early as July of 1898 he had been in favor of a coaling station under the American flag and with a sufficient military force to maintain the authority of the Stars and Stripes.[1] Later, when the peace treaty came under discussion in the Senate, he explained his partiality for acquisition on the ground that it meant the taking of an important step in the advancement of America, commercially and otherwise. The Senator predicted that the partition of China would shut off America from that vast market unless she utilized the opportunity of gaining a foothold in the Orient offered to her by the terms of the pace treaty.[2]

Senator S. B. Elkins, of West Virginia, scanned the future and let his thoughts dwell on America's prospects, not for a century only but for thousands of years. The results of American work in the conquered territories over such a long stretch of time, the Senator confidently expected to be as gratifying as those that had followed the annexations after the Mexican War.[3]

Another Senator who may be classed as a trade expansionist was J. B. Foraker, of Ohio. On August 7, 1898 he was quoted as saying that the United States had a divine mission to perform and that the scope of such a mission included freeing the Philippines from the "Spanish yoke" and the "midnight darkness" to which they had been subjected. However, he did not omit to mention extended commerce as America's future need. Forty per cent of her manufactured products, he thought, should be marketed abroad and the place for those products was "in the Far East."[4] During the debate on the treaty, Senator Foraker

[1] *N. Y. Times*, July 31, 1898, p. 1.

[2] *Ibid.*, January 26, 1899, p. 1.

[3] *Cong. Record*, 57th Cong., 1st Sess., p. 211.

[4] *N. Y. Times*, August 7, 1898, p. 1.

delivered a carefuly reasoned speech on the power of the American government to acquire and govern territory without limitations.[1] Three years later, he affirmed that the commercial side had a great deal to do with the acquisition and continued retention of the Philippines. And after pointing out the commercial and strategic value of a port in the Orient, he said:

> . . . I have always believed that in acquiring the Philippines by that treaty, that in ratifying that treaty, that in taking possession, that in continuing to occupy and hold and govern the Philippines, we have been acting not mistakenly or unwisely, but just the opposite.[2]

The name of Senator W. P. Frye, of Maine, one of the Peace Commissioners, also figured among the expansionists. From a religious and spiritual standpoint he could not " view with equanimity " the restoration of the Philippine Islands to Spain or their partition among other Powers. Rejection of the treaty further meant losing Manila and " all the vast advantages acquired through the war in the Far East." [3] During the election campaign in 1900, Senator Frye wished to keep the Islands in order to give their people " freedom and liberty under the law, and for the commercial interests of the 75,000,000 of people " in America. He was an expansionist, and remembering that Thomas Jefferson had been the first to give impulse to expansionism, he rejoiced that he was in such good company.[4]

Still another powerful advocate of expansion appeared in the person of Senator M. A Hanna of Ohio, the close friend and adviser of President McKinley. On July 31,

[1] *Cong. Record*, 55th Cong., 3rd Sess., pp. 563-570.

[2] *Cong. Record*, 57th Cong., 1st Sess., pp. 5293-5294.

[3] *N. Y. Times*, January 29, 1899, p. 5.

[4] *N. Y. Daily Tribune*, October 27, 1900, p. 3.

1898, Senator Hanna urged careful deliberation in handling the Philippine question. "We at least want," he said, "a footing on those islands. Although there may be a sentiment against keeping them, there is a bigger sentiment against giving them back to Spain. We are confronted with new conditions today, and we intend to work out the problems in a manner which will be for the best interests of the country."[1] And in the presence of citizens of Norfolk, Nebraska, during the compaign of 1900, Senator Hanna, taking up the issue of imperialism, asserted a determination not to haul down the flag while American dead lay buried on Philippine soil. "If it is commercialism," he declared, "to want the possession of a strategic point giving the American people an opportunity to maintain a foothold in the markets of that great Eastern country, for God's sake let us have comercialism."[2]

While Senator Nelson, of Minnesota, confined his observations during the treaty debate to the constitutional power of the United States to acquire and hold colonies permanently,[3] three years later he gave utterance to his belief in the immense commercial value of the Philippines, situated in the center of "a great beehive of humanity." The Boxer rebellion, in his opinion, fully showed the advantage in holding the Islands for the protection of Americans and American interests in the Orient.[4]

More frankly specific than the rest of his colleagues, Senator J. C. Pritchard showed in several speeches that he was fully alive to the bond of union that should bind the cotton manufacturers of the South to the vast markets of the East. "The thing which the Southern people need

[1] *N. Y. Times*, July 31, 1898, p. 1.

[2] *N. Y. Daily Tribune*, October 20, 1900, p. 14.

[3] *Cong. Record*, 55th Cong., 3rd Sess., pp. 831-838.

[4] *Cong. Record*, 57th Cong., 1st Sess., p. 1979.

above all others," he affirmed, " is a market for their surplus cotton and cotton fabrics, and the Orient is the principal section whose people are by climate and habits the natural customers of the cotton planters of the South." [1] So, appreciating the weight of this argument, the North Carolina Senator declared that " those of us who live in the South can not afford to give our sanction to any policy which undertakes to permit these islands to pass from under our control as a nation." [2]

Senator W. M. Stewart, a Silverite Senator from Nevada, argued for ratification in order to give the American people time to decide. He did not believe that all the reasons for retention had been given. He did not take much stock in the fear that American institutions would be imperiled by the acquisition of the Archipelago. He appreciated the value of Oriental trade, desired employment for unemployed pedagogues in America, and opportunity in business for enterprising young men in the United States.[3] A few years later, he expressed the conviction that the Philippines would prove more valuable than could at that time be conceived, and that those islands were " going to add more wealth in the way of trade and commerce to the United States " than any other possible acquisition.[4] " I believe," he continued, " the acquisition of those islands will redound to the benefit of the United States and of the people thereof. It will make markets, it will create commerce, and we will civilize the people and do them good." [5]

The desire for a coaling station found lodgment in the

[1] *Cong. Record*, 57th Cong., 1st Sess., p. 2094.

[2] *Ibid.*

[3] *Cong. Record*, 55th Cong., 3rd Sess., pp. 1735-1736, 1832.

[4] *Cong. Record*, 57th Cong., 1st Sess., p. 1093.

[5] *Ibid.*, p. 5349.

mind of Senator Thurston, of Nebraska, as early as the first week of August, 1898.[1]

No better summary of the arguments in favor of ratification of the peace treaty can be found than that contained in the speeches of Senator Lodge who marshalled with equal success the moral, the material, and the other more or less metaphysical reasons for expansion.

He touched the chord stressing America's responsibility, and these were his words:

> . . . I can look at this question in only one way. A great responsibility has come to us. If we are unfit for it and unequal to it, then we should shirk it and fly from it. But I believe that we are both fit and capable, and that therefore we should meet it and take it up.[2]

But to Mr. Lodge's way of thinking the opportunity was as inviting as the responsibility was pressing. He, therefore, went on and said:

> There is much else involved here, vast commercial and trade interests, which I believe we have a right to guard and a duty to foster. But the opponents of the treaty have placed their opposition on such high and altruistic grounds that I have preferred to meet him [*sic*] there, and not to discuss the enormous material benefits to our trade, our industries, and our labor dependent upon a right settlement of this question, both directly and indirectly.[3]

A year after the ratification of the treaty, Senator Lodge believed as firmly as before that the care of American interests coincided with her moral obligations in the Philippine question. On March 7, 1900, he said:

[1] *New York Times*, August 7, 1898, p. 1.

[2] *Cong. Record*, 55th Cong., 3rd Sess., p. 960.

[3] *Ibid.*, p. 960.

. . . I believe we are in the Philippines as righteously as we are there rightfully and legally. I believe that to abandon the islands . . . would be a wrong to humanity, a dereliction of duty, a base betrayal of the Filipinos who have supported us . . . and in the highest degree contrary to sound morals. As to the expediency, the arguments in favor of the retention of the Philippines seem to me so overwhelming that I should regard their loss as a calamity to our trade and commerce and to all our business interests so great that no man can measure it.[1]

These reasons of expediency must have troubled Senator Lodge's conscience for he added later on these words:

I do not myself consider them sordid, for anything which involves the material interests and the general welfare of the people of the United States seems to me of the highest merit and the greatest importance. Whatever duty to others might seem to demand, I should pause long before supporting any policy if there were the slightest suspicion that it was not for the benefit of the people of the United States. I conceive my first duty to be always to the American people, and I have ever considered it the cardinal principle of American statesmanship to advocate policies which would operate for the benefit of the people of the United States. . . .[2]

The trade argument found its clearest exposition in Senator Lodge's keynote speech as chairman of the Republican National Convention in 1900. On June 20 of that year, in Philadelphia, he spoke as follows:

We make no hypocritical pretense of being interested in the Philippines solely on account of others. While we regard the welfare of those people as a sacred trust, we regard the welfare of the American people first. We see our duty to our-

[1] *Cong. Record*, 56th Cong., 1st Sess., p. 2618.

[2] *Ibid.*, p. 2627.

selves as well as to others. We believe in trade expansion. By every legitimate means within the province of government and legislation we mean to stimulate the expansion of our trade and to open new markets. Greatest of all markets is China. Our trade there is growing by leaps and bounds. Manila, the prize of war, gives us inestimable advantages in developing that trade. It is the cornerstone of our Eastern policy, and the brilliant diplomacy of John Hay in securing from all nations a guarantee of our treaty rights, and of the open door in China rests upon it.[1]

THE METAPHYSICAL GROUP

Four Senators gave reasons for their vote for the peace treaty which were more or less vague and dogmatic. Senator Fairbanks, of Indiana, regarded it as America's paramount duty to consider the obligations which "one of the great evolutions of human history" had imposed on her.[2] Senator J. T. Morgan, of Alabama, declared that he gave his vote for the treaty because that course was essentially right. Such course was essentially right because any other course would have been essentially wrong.[3] But even if Senator Morgan was so stern and unbending in his determination to follow what was ethically right, he was not entirely blind to arguments less exalted. He thought that, next to the treaty of Guadalupe Hidalgo, the treaty of Paris was the most advantageous which the United States had concluded in the nineteenth century and he was not unaware of the peculiar importance it had for the people of the Southern states.[4] Senator O. H. Platt, of Connecticut, sounded a solemn note. He believed Providence had

[1] *New York Tribune*, June 21, 1900, pt. ii, p. 2.

[2] *Cong. Record*, 57th Cong., 1st Sess., pp. 2096-2097; see also the *New York Times*, February 7, 1899.

[3] *Cong. Record*, 57th Cong., 1st Sess., pp. 6084-6085.

[4] *Cong. Record*, 56th Cong., 1st Sess., p. 6019.

brought a challenge to America's concept of duty. That situation was but a part of the onward sweep of the "great force of Christian civilization." The same force had been responsible for the great event on Plymouth Rock, had stood behind the infantry at Santiago and the ships on Manila Bay. In Senator Platt's opinion, America had been chosen to carry on the work of human betterment.[1] Senator E. O. Wolcott, of Colorado, had a theory that ran much along the same channels. He trusted the judgment of the peace commissioners and the government. He was not sure but that America had reached a point in her national evolution where "Anglo-Saxon restlessness" was irresistibly stimulated to plant the American flag in an archipelago which "inevitable destiny" had proffered.

But the classical statement of this faith in sublimated dogmatism appeared in a speech of Senator Lodge on March 7, 1900. His words were these:

Like every great nation, we have come more than once in our history to where the road of fate divided. Thus far we have never failed to take the right path. Again are we come to the parting of the ways. Again a momentous choice is offered to us. Shall we hesitate and make in coward fashion what Dante calls "the great refusal"? Even now we can abandon the Monroe Doctrine, we can reject the Pacific, we can shut ourselves up between our oceans, as Switzerland is inclosed among her hills, and then it would be inevitable that we should sink out from among the great powers of the world and heap up riches that some stronger and bolder people, who do not fear their fate, might gather them. Or we may follow the true laws of our being, the laws in obedience to which we have come to be what we are, and then we shall stretch out into the Pacific; we shall stand in the front rank of the world powers; we shall give to our labor and our industry new and larger and better

[1] *Cong. Record*, 55th Cong., 3rd Sess., p. 287.

opportunities; we shall prosper ourselves; we shall benefit mankind. What we have done was inevitable because it was in accordance with the laws of our being as a nation, in the defiance and disregard of which lie ruin and retreat.[1]

SUMMARY

To summarize: Of the thirty Senators whose views have been examined, seven voted for the treaty because they were for the establishment of peace conditions and against a renewal of negotiations or, possibly, of war; three voted as they did because they thought or had been assured that the American Government and people could be trusted to frown upon colonial systems; twelve Senatorial minds were attracted by the variegated hues of expansionism; four Senators were oppressed and stimulated by some mysterious force, and dwelt continuously on "inevitable destiny", and the "laws of a nation's being"; one Senator,[2] though against annexation, voted for the treaty in obedience to instructions from his state legislature;[3] and three Senators thought a vote for the treaty was a patriotic duty in view of the outbreak of hostilities in the Philippines.

These thirty votes were made up of twenty-one Republican, five Democratic, one Populist, and three Silverite Senators. Of the twenty-one Republicans, two had the peace motive, three were for a subsequent definition of policy, one desired to support the flag because it had been fired upon, eleven were expansionists, three were believers in the philosophy of inevitable destiny, and one voted in obedience to the expressed will of the legislature of his state. Of the five Democrats, three had the peace motive, one the desire to uphold the flag, and only one was a deter-

[1] *Cong. Record*, 56th Cong., 1st Sess., p. 2530.

[2] Senator G. C. Perkins of California.

[3] See *N. Y. Times*, January 4, 1899, p. 5 and January 21, 1899, p. 4.

minist. The lone populist voted out of a desire for peace. One Silverite Senator wanted peace, one had the flag-motive, and the third was a convinced expansionist. The twenty-seven Senators who voted for the peace treaty but remained silent as to their reasons consisted of eighteen Republicans, two Populists, five Democrats, one Silverite, and one Independent.

But whatever motive may have operated most powerfully among the Senators at the particular time, there is little doubt that to all or almost all of them the "cardinal principle of American statesmanship" was to "advocate policies which would operate for the benefit of the people of the United States".[1]

[1] Quoted from Senator Lodge's speech, *Cong. Record*, 56th *Cong.*, 1st Sess., p. 2627.

CHAPTER III

The Constitutional Relation of the Philippines to the United States

The Spanish-American War marked a new period in American history. That struggle resulted in America's self-recognition of her place in the ranks of the world Powers, the annexation of territory for which there was very little probability of incorporation as units in the American system of the " States United ", and the revelation of an unsuspected element of America's national psychology—the willingness to shoulder the responsibilities of empire-building and the white man's burden. Interesting in itself, those facts became more so when the peculiarities of the American system of government had to be reconciled to the existence of a colonial system.

For a hundred years the United States had been constantly expanding its territorial area in the American continent over sparsely inhabited regions, all of which were capable of assimilation to her body politic. These territories had but to await the arrival of frontiersmen and pioneer settlers in numbers sufficient for admission as equal members of the " Union of States "

Over this broad land was the authority of a national government whose powers were derived from the American constitution—an instrument of government drafted amidst an atmosphere of profound distrust of governments and providing for the exercise of enumerated governmental powers. In the two years following the close of the war with Spain the issue was plainly presented whether or not under such a system there was room for the acquiring of territory to be held and governed as colonies.[1] While there may have been great divergence of opinion as to the period during which America would remain in control of all or some of the territories ceded by Spain in 1899, there seemed to be reasonable unanimity in the belief that the possibility of the ultimate admission of such territories to statehood in the Union was an unlikely and undesirable contingency.[2] The reasons were obvious. These new possessions were non-contiguous territories and were inhabited by people entirely different in culture, customs and civilization. If they were not to be admitted as states, the remaining alternatives were either separation or the status, temporary or permanent, of colonial dependencies. During the period of such a temporary or permanent connection the constitutional question was: Would the Constitution apply in its entirety to the new dependencies?

THE CASES OF DE LIMA *v.* BIDWELL AND THE FOURTEEN DIAMOND RINGS

These legal questions came up before the Supreme Court in what is commonly termed the Insular Cases. Those cases arose out of the carrying on of trade and commerce between the United States and these new possessions. Products coming from the latter were subjected to the rates of the Dingley tariff which levied duties on goods from "foreign countries". Almost immediately, therefore, the question arose whether Porto Rico and the Philippines were

[1] See Resolution of Senator Vest, of December 6, 1898, quoted in Latané, *America as a World Power*, p. 75.

[2] See Schurman "Philippine Affairs, A Retrospect and Outlook", an address before Cornell University, quoted in part in Malcolm's *Government of the P. I.*, p. 1335, and the McEnery Resolution, *Cong. Record*, 55th Cong., 3rd Sess., p. 1847.

"foreign countries" within the meaning of the tariff Act of 1897 and their products subject to its schedule of duties. The Supreme Court passed upon this question in the case of De Lima *v.* Bidwell[1] for Porto Rico and that of the Fourteen Diamond Rings[2] for the Philippines.

In the first case, De Lima and Company imported sugar from Porto Rico to the port of New York in 1899 after the ratification of the Treaty of Paris and before the passage of the Porto-Rican Act of 1900.[3] The collector of customs of the port levied the full rate of the Dingley rates on this shipment of sugar. De Lima and Company brought suit for the recovery of the sum paid as import dues and appealed the case from the United States Circuit Court for the Southern district of New York to the Federal Supreme Court.

In the Fourteen Diamond Rings case, the facts were as follows: E. J. Pepke, a citizen of the United States, enlisted in the army at the outbreak of the war with Spain and was sent with his regiment to the island of Luzon in the Philippine group. While in that island and subsequent to the ratification of the treaty of peace, he acquired possession of fourteen diamond rings. He took the diamond rings with him when he sailed, in obedience to orders, on the 31st of July, 1899 for San Francisco on an army transport. On September 25, 1899 he obtained his discharge from the army and later proceeded to Chicago, where the rings were seized by a customs officer as having been unlawfully brought into the United States.[4]

[1] 182 *U. S. Reports*, 1.

[2] 183 *U. S. Reports*, 176.

[3] *Insular Cases*, Gov't Printing Office, 1901, p. 609; also 182 *U. S. Reports*, 2.

[4] *Insular Cases*, Gov't Printing Office, 1901, p. 307.

It will be seen that the issue which was raised in the two cases was whether or not goods imported from Porto Rico and the Philippines were to be regarded as having come from "foreign countries" within the meaning of the U. S. Tariff law. Did Porto Rico and the Philippines cease to be "foreign countries" after the ratification of the treaty with Spain? If international law recognized them as parts of the United States, would the same thing hold true from the point of view of the constitutional law of the United States? In other words, does the Constitution immediately become operative in newly acquired territory?

Those holding the view that all the provisions of the Constitution were operative argued that the claim of power outside of the Constitution and, therefore unlimited, was contrary to the American theory of government; that the theory of incorporation being necessary to make the Constitution operative in territory held by the United States was unsound; that the express injunctions contained in the provisions of the Constitution were applicable everywhere within the territory of the United States; that among these injunctions were those contained in Art. I, Section 9 of the Constitution providing for uniformity "throughout the United States" of "all duties, imposts, and excises" and the amendments guaranteeing civil rights to individuals; that Article IX of the Treaty of Paris giving Congress the power to "determine the civil rights and political status of the native inhabitants of the territories" ceded by Spain could not invalidate, even if it did conflict with, these provisions of the Constitution; that the plain meaning of the term "throughout the United States" used in that section of the Constitution prescribing uniform duties, imposts, and excises embraced all territory within the jurisdiction of the United States; and that the words "imported from foreign countries" used in the Tariff Act of 1897, clearly, could not apply to products imported from Porto Rico and the Philippines.[1]

In answer to these propositions, the government maintained that the power to acquire territory was an inherent, sovereign right as well as one derived from the constitutional power to make war and conclude treaties; that the power to govern territories was implied in the power to acquire them; that this power was specifically granted and solely controlled by that provision empowering Congress to "dispose of and make all needful rules and regulations respecting the territory or other property belonging to the United States"; [2] that the clause of the Constitution requiring duties, imposts and excises to be uniform throughout the United States does not apply to the new possessions, for the term "United States" here meant the "States United" in the Union; that the Constitution can not extend of its own force over acquired territory; and that the spirit in which the Constitution should be interpreted ought to be one in which the practical element should determine in doubtful cases.[3]

To the question thus posed the Court decided in the leading case of De Lima *v.* Bidwell [4] by a five to four vote that Porto Rico (and therefore, inferentially, the other insular possessions) is not "a foreign country within the meaning of the tariff laws but a territory of the United States . . . ." [5] declared that the right to acquire ter-

[1] *The Insular Cases*, Gov't Printing Office, 1901, p. 45; also 182 *U. S.*, pp. 19-94.

[2] Article iv, sec. iii, par. 4.

[3] P. 144 of the *Insular Cases*, Gov't Printing Office, 1901; 182 *U. S.*, pp. 74-94.

[4] 182 *U. S.*, 1.

[5] *Ibid.*, p. 200.

ritory involves the right to govern and dispose of it.[1] The opinion went on further and said:

Territory thus acquired can remain a foreign territory under the tariff laws only upon one of two theories: either that the word "foreign" applies to such countries as were foreign at the time the statute was enacted, notwithstanding any subsequent change in their condition, or that they remain foreign under the tariff laws until Congress has formally embraced them within the customs union of the States.[2]

The majority of the justices held these alternatives to be inadmissible and defined a foreign country as one "exclusively within the sovereignty of a foreign nation, and without the sovereignty of the United States."[3] These principles were reaffirmed and applied to the Philippines in the Fourteen Diamond Rings case.[4] They rendered inoperative the duties which up to that time had been imposed under the Dingley Act.

THE DOWNES *v.* BIDWELL CASE

By the Foraker Act of April 12, 1900[5] and the Philippines Tariff Act of March 8, 1902[6] Congress imposed the regular rates of the Dingley Tariff less a reduction of 85 per cent on products coming from Porto Rico and 25 per cent on those imported from the Philippines. This presented the issue whether Congress, in creating this tariff on goods coming from America's insular possessions, did not thereby violate the provision of the Constitution requiring

[1] 182 *U. S.*, p. 196.
[2] *Ibid.*, p. 197.
[3] *Ibid.*, p. 180.
[4] 183 *U. S.*, p. 176.
[5] *U. S. Stat. L.*, vol. xxxi, p. 77.
[6] *U. S. Stat. L.*, vol. xxxii, pt. i, p. 54.

all "duties, imposts, and excises to be uniform throughout the United States."[1] The question came up in the concrete when Downes and Company sought to recover the duties paid by them under the Foraker Act to the collector of customs of New York on a shipment of oranges from Porto Rico to that port. This case was decided on the same day as the De Lima case[2] and decided in a way that seemed to stretch the elasticity of legal formulas to the breaking point. The opinion of the court handed down by Mr. Justice Brown sought to show a distinction between those provisions of the Constitution that "go to the very root of the power of Congress to act at all, irrespective of time or place, and such as are operative only throughout the United States, or among the several states."[3] It held that section prescribing uniformity of imposts, duties, and excises to be operative only within the several states and declared Porto Rico to be, although not a foreign territory within the meaning of the general tariff act,[4] one that was merely appurtenant to, and not a part of the United States within the meaning of the revenue clauses of the Constitution.[5] The other justices who concurred with Mr. Justice Brown did so on grounds that were clearly different from those assumed by the latter. Chief-Justice Fuller in his dissenting opinion said:

> . . . the contention seems to be that if an organized and settled province of another sovereignty is acquired by the United States, Congress has the power to keep it like a disembodied shade, in an intermediate state of ambiguous existence for an

[1] Article I, Section 8 of the Constitution.

[2] See 182 *U. S.*, p. 1 and 182 *U. S.*, p. 244.

[3] 182 *U. S.*, p. 244.

[4] De Lima *v.* Bidwell.

[5] *Ibid.*

indefinite period; and, more than that, that after it has been called from that limbo, commerce with it is absolutely subject to the will of Congress, irrespective of constitutional provisions.[1]

THE CASE OF U. S. *v.* BULL

The principle of the Downes case was adopted by the Philippine Supreme Court when that body passed upon the case of the United States *v.* Bull.[2] H. N. Bull was master of a Norwegian steam sailing vessel which arrived in Manila with a shipment of cattle and other animals from Formosa. Charged with violating various acts of the Philippine Commission[3] penalizing cruelty to animals while in transit, H. N. Bull questioned the constitutionality of these acts which were made to apply to all vessels plying from one port in the Philippine Islands to another, or from any foreign port to any port within the Philippine Islands. Disregarding the international aspect of the case, the point in question was whether or not it was competent and constitutional for the Philippine Commission which was the creature of an Act of Congress[4] to perform the legislative functions that were exercised in the enactment of these laws. Did these Commission statutes interfere with the power given to Congrss over interstate and foreign commerce?

In arriving at its decision the highest court of the Philippines followed in the footsteps of the United States Supreme Court, declaring in effect, that a formal act of incorporation was necessary to extend the Constitution of the

[1] 182 *U. S.*, p. 372.

[2] 15 *Philippine Reports*, p. 7. See also the Dorr Case, 195 *U. S.*, p. 138. For a later Porto Rico case, see Balzac *v.* P. R., 258 *U. S.*, p. 298.

[3] Act no. 55 of Jan. 1, 1909 and no. 275 of Oct. 23, 1901.

[4] Act of July 1, 1902.

United States over acquired territory.[1] The Philippine court found the charter for the government of the islands not in the constitution but in the "formally and legally expressed will of the President and Congress." "The authority for its [the Philippine Government] creation and maintenance," the court said, "is derived from the Constitution of the United States, which, however, operates on the President and Congress, and not directly on the Philippine government." [2]

It might be well to summarize the specific points that were covered by these four cases thus far examined. The De Lima and Fourteen Diamond Rings cases decided that import duties may not be levied on goods coming from insular possessions to the United States under those provisions of the tariff law levying duties on goods imported from "foreign countries." These decisions found Porto Rico and the Philippines to be domestic territories.[3] These court pronouncements automatically destroyed the barrier against the products of Porto Rico and the Philippines that was represented by the dues under the general tariff act, which was declared inoperative. Congress legislated and imposed lower duties than before on Porto-Rican and Philippine goods, thus re-creating to the extent of those duties the barrier that had been demolished by the reasoning of the judicial mind. The constitutionality of this procedure came before the Supreme Court of the United States in the case of Downes *v.* Bidwell and the Philippine Supreme Court in that of United States *v.* Bull. Contrary to what might have been expected, the learned Justices discovered that the Constitution did not, in its entirety, apply

[1] 15 *Philippine Reports*, pp. 21, 22.

[2] *Ibid.*, p. 27.

[3] *Supra*, pp. 50, 51.

to the unincorporated territories of the United States and that its uniformity of duties clause was to be enforced only within the system of States and whatever territory Congress might choose to incorporate and include as coming within the scope of this and similar clauses.[1] Commenting on the decision in the Downes case Professor Burgess said:

> . . . the decision . . . was based by four of the justices upon a principle which a majority of the court had already repudiated in the De Lima case, and by one of the justices upon a principle the other eight repudiated in the Downes case; while the dissenting opinion in the Downes case by Chief Justice Fuller and Justices Harlan, Brewer, and Peckham was based upon the principle which had been pronounced sound and valid in the De Lima decision.[2]

THE ECONOMIC ASPECT OF THE INSULAR CASES

It is evident from what has already been said that these cases abound in fine-spun, legal distinctions which are so dear to those with a bent for disputation. That is not, however, the aspect which is of concern to us. Were these wordy legal battles fought merely for the joy of fighting, from an admiration of the display of legal acumen, or an enthusiastic and faithful adherence to the desire to maintain a government of "laws and not of men?" Beside the legal side of these cases, there was another one which was quite as important. On the abstract legal question whether the Constitution follows the flag men might differ and differ seriously. The answer to such a query in pure

[1] *Supra*, pp. 51, 52.

[2] *Pol. Science Quarterly*, Sept., 1901, vol. xvi, no. 3, p. 492. For other magazine articles on these cases see G. F. Edmunds in *North American Review*, Aug., 1901, p. 149; S. E. Baldwin, "The Insular Cases," *Yale Review*, Aug., 1901 and C. F. Randolph in *Columbia Law Review*, Nov., 1901.

logic, nevertheless, can at best produce nothing but a fleeting sense of intellectual satisfaction. Much more important and of far greater consequence was the corollary to the legal question involved. If the Constitution followed the flag, and paragraph 1 of the eighth section of its first article requiring uniformity of duties throughout the United States were applied, Congress could not impose protective duties on products brought into continental United States from its tropical possessions.

In his argument before the Supreme Court on these cases, the Attorney-General of the United States spoke of the annexations resulting from the war with Spain as but an additional incident in the expansion of the American nation. He saw in Jefferson's purchase of Louisiana a "commercial and patriotically selfish idea." [1]

Referring to that clause of the Constitution giving Congress the power to "dispose of and make all needful rules and regulations respecting the territory or other property belonging to the United States," the chief legal officer of the government assigned its authorship to Gouverneur Morris and quoted him as having written a letter in 1803 in which he said:

> I always thought that when we should acquire Canada and Louisiana it would be proper to govern them as provinces and allow them no voice in our councils. In wording the third section of the fourth article I went as far as circumstances would permit to establish the exclusion. Candor obliges me to add my belief that had it been more pointedly expressed a strong opposition would have been made.[2]

Sketching his historico-legal argument, the Attorney-General continued:

[1] *The Insular Cases*, a volume containing the briefs, arguments, etc. of those cases (Gov't Printing Office, 1901), p. 282.

[2] *The Insular Cases*, p. 282.

. . . the point I desire to make here is, that at the bottom of these acquisitions of territory, at the bottom of that clause of the Constitution which authorized the government of the acquisition, lay the material, the commercial, the expansive idea of the thrifty, progressive, active American, the pioneer spirit that, pressing onward from frontier to frontier, went out to reduce and conquer territory for their own use and benefit. I propose to argue that when our forefathers made the Constitution they made it as States, or as the people of the States.[1]

And his peroration in this argument on behalf of the government, ran thus:

We have not sought a doctrine which by subtle disputation would entangle and embarrass. We have remembered that a great world power, extending its domain from the frozen seas on the North to where the encircling palm trees grow in the Pacific islands, must not be bound by rules too strict or too confining; that what might tend toward progress and development in one place might only hamper in another. Therefore we have sought an interpretation which should continue in the legislative body which represents the American people that wise and sound discretion which it would be a slander and an imputation upon our country for a moment to believe they would not always exercise. . . . [2]

These economic portions of the Attorney-General's argument were supplemented and re-enforced by a brief written on behalf of several industries in the United States before the Supreme Court.[3] It was filed on behalf of individuals who claimed to be "as deeply interested in the final determination of the question involved as the Government itself." "A decision in these cases adverse to the Government," the brief went on,

[1] *The Insular Cases*, p. 282.

[2] *Ibid.*, p. 338.

[3] *Ibid.*, pp. 239 *et seq.*

would make it possible not only to suddenly endanger our revenues upon a mere cession of acquired territory—no man can say to what extent—without the consent of Congress, but it would jeopard [*sic*] a very large amount of capital invested in the States in certain agricultural industries, the protection and development of which it has long been the policy of the Government to safeguard in our customs-revenue laws. These industries embracing tobacco, sugar, rice, hemp, fruits, etc., cannot compete on the unequal terms which would be forced upon them with like products grown in ceded tropical possessions. No one can now say to what extent the United States may go or feel required to go, through the fortunes of war, in taking over ceded possessions. No one would have been bold enough to assert, at the inception of our last war, that a cession of Porto Rico and of the Philippines would be one of the results. Eventually Cuba may be taken in to safeguard our interests, or her people may finally vote for annexation. This case is far-reaching in its possible consequences to our fiscal, industrial, and labor interests. Heretofore our cessions have been of contiguous territory having scanty products and comparatively few people, who could be readily assimilated, etc. We have now other and serious conditions to deal with. The Union was of States for their protection first; and not, as too many seem to suppose, for the exercise of charity toward inhabitants who might or might not come to us by war.[1]

Translated into economic terms, the real question in the Insular cases becomes one of the constitutional power of Congress to throw around certain industries in the continental area of the United States the advantages of a protective tariff even as against products of territory also within the domain of the American government. The novelty of the problem consisted in the need for the reconciliation of imperialism and protection. The party that sponsored the annexations was also the party of protection. In 1900

[1] *The Insular Cases*, pp. 239 *et seq.*

that party had said, under the heading of "The Porto Rican Act and the Beet Sugar Question:"

The first thought which came to the minds of the farmers when the events following the war for the liberation of Cuba brought under our control certain tropical areas was whether or not the possession or control of tropical territory by the United States would injure or perhaps destroy the opportunities which they believe they had almost within their grasp for supplying the $100,000,000 worth of sugar which the people of the United States annually consume. The fear — if it reached the stage in which it could be called by that name — was answered in the negative by the Republican party when it passed the Porto Rican bill. . . . In other words, it was a distinct promise to the farmer that he need not fear that the Republican party would permit the cheap labor and cheap sugar of any tropical territory to be brought in a manner which would destroy the infant industry of beet sugar production which the farmers of the United States have, under the fostering care of the Republican party, been building up during the last few years.[1]

In 1904 the plank on protection to American industries in the Republican platform declared the principle of protection which "guards and develops" American industries to be "a cardinal policy of the Republican party." The extent of such protection was to be measured by the difference in the cost of production at home and abroad.[2]

In 1908 the Republican party volume became still more definite and favored a free interchange of products between the Philippines and the United States with "such limitations as to sugar and tobacco as will afford adequate protection to domestic interests."[3] Throughout this period

[1] *Republican Campaign Textbook*, 1900, p. 152.

[2] *Republican Campaign Textbook*, 1904, p. 486.

[3] *Republican Campaign Textbook*, 1908, p. 462.

the party that made these expressions of policy was in control of the executive and legislative branches of the government and these declarations may therefore be taken as a fairly authoritive index of governmental policy. How authoritative they were will be revealed in the subsequent provisions of the economic legislation enacted, as well as in the debates attending the passage of such legislation.

The elections of 1912 transferred governmental control to the Democratic party. The Philippine plank of the victorious Democrats reaffirmed their previous stand against a policy of "imperialism and colonial exploitation," favored the "immediate declaration of the nation's purpose to recognize" the independence of the Philippine Islands as soon as a stable government could be established, declared for an American guarantee until a treaty of neutralization could be secured, and provided for the retention of "such land as may be necessary for coaling stations and naval bases." [1]

After this sketchy outline of the background for the economic legislation that was subsequently enacted, it may not be amiss to attempt the difficult task of correlating the economic with the other factors that went into the making of what was to be the history of the ensuing twenty years of Philippine-American relations after the Spanish-American war. When the question of the acquisition of the Philippines came before the American government for decision, President McKinley, in his letter of instructions to the American peace commissioners at Paris, defined the attitude of the administration in the following terms:

Without any original thought of complete or even partial acquisition, the presence and success of our arms at Manila imposes upon us obligations which we cannot disregard. The march of events rules and overrules human action. Avowing

[1] *Democratic Campaign Textbook*, 1912. p. 30.

unreservedly the purpose which has animated all our effort, and still solicitous to adhere to it, we cannot be unmindful that, without any design or desire on our part, the war has brought us new duties and responsibilities which we must meet and discharge as becomes a great nation on whose growth and career from the beginning the Ruler of Nations has plainly written the high command and pledge of civilization. Incidental to our tenure in the Philippines is the commercial opportunity to which American statesmanship cannot be indifferent. It is just to use every legitimate means for the enlargement of American trade; but we seek no advantages in the Orient which are not common to all. Asking only the open door for ourselves, we are ready to accord the open door to others. The commercial opportunity which is naturally and inevitably associated with this new opening depends less on large territorial possession than upon an adequate commercial basis and upon broad and equal privileges.[1]

This mosaic of motives reflected in these instructions faithfully represents public opinion on any question of public interest. Issues that are thrust into the forefront of public attention and to which a yes or no answer is required have the effect of welding ludicrously dissimilar elements into a temporarily cohesive group. A community of interest for the moment serves as the binding tie. The minute the desired step has been taken, new alignments are needed as each interested factor strives to deflect the course of events to suit its own theories. Subsequent events are simply the registered results of the momentary supremacy of one or more of those factors.

Viewed in this light, the decisions in the insular cases constituted a distinct victory for the economic interests.[2] "The judgment in the Downes case," wrote Professor

[1] Quoted in Latané, *American as a World Power*, pp. 70-71.

[2] *Supra*, pp. 50-54.

Burgess, "is therefore, nothing but an arbitrary bit of patchwork. Its purpose is to satisfy a certain demand of fancied political expediency. . . ." [1]

The views of another scholar are also not without interest. "The status of the new annexations," said Latané, "was practically settled, on commercial and political grounds, before the constitutional questions involved came up for adjudication. The dominant business interests of the country were opposed to the full incorporation of the new possessions, the public opinion decided the question that way. When it came to the test the American nation, despite the charges of inconsistency, applied to the situation the doctrine of inferior races and denied to the inhabitants of Porto Rico and the Philippines equal rights under the Constitution. The Supreme Court could not have reversed the decision of the American people, where such far-reaching acts of the president and of Congress were involved, without creating serious confusion. Consequently they bowed their heads before *un fait accompli*." [2]

This, then is the significance of the Insular Cases: They gave to the policy-making branch of the government, that is to say,—Congress—practically unhampered power in the government of the new possessions. Thenceforth Congress could, if it chose, make imperialism and its consequences as sweet a dose as it could possibly be made and keep away from the American people or American economic interests that which was distasteful and bitter. The Supreme Court adopted an interpretation which, in the words of the Attorney-General, continued "in the great legislative body which represents the American people that wise and sound discretion which it would be a slander and an imputation

[1] *Pol. Science Quarterly*, September, 1901, p. 504.

[2] Latané, *America as a World Power*, pp. 151-152; see also Beard, *Contemporary American History*, pp. 213, 218-220.

upon our country for a moment to believe they would not always exercise. . . ." [1]

Two years after these words were spoken, R. F. Hoxie wrote a realistic article on "American Colonial Policy and the Tariff." [2] By that time the Customs Tariff Act of 1901 had been enacted for the Philippines by the United States Philippine Commission.[3] Mr. Hoxie saw in this tariff act an exercise by the Philippine Commission of "the right to use the tariff as a means for trade discrimination against colonial possessions." [4] He espied danger not from the "collusion but from the clash of selfish interests." Previous to the annexations, there were, he said, two determined factions. One consisted of the exporting industries and wanted government action to broaden their markets abroad. The other was composed of the protected industries and was determined to oppose concessions to foreign goods in the home market. But when it came to the subject of trade with the new territories after their annexation and after the decision in the Downes case, the opportunity for satisfying the demands of both factions arose. "The logical result now was," said Mr. Hoxie, "free entry of our goods into the subject territory to satisfy the first faction and a tariff against the goods of the dependency to satisfy the second." [5] Whether Mr. Hoxie's logic in this instance did or did not coincide very well with the logic of later history will be seen in our succeeding inquiries.

[1] *The Insular Cases*, Gov't Printing Office, 1901, p. 338.

[2] *The Journal of Political Economy*, March, 1903, p. 198.

[3] *Infra*, ch. iv.

[4] *The Journal of Political Economy*, March, 1903, p. 217.

[5] *The Journal of Political Economy*, March, 1903, p. 248.

CHAPTER IV

Tariff on Goods Imported into the Philippine Islands

THE CUSTOMS TARIFF UP TO NOVEMBER 15, 1901

The Fourteen Diamond Rings case which finally determined the constitutional status of the Philippines as well as the limitation or, rather, lack of limitation, on the powers of Congress over the islands was not decided until 1901. Foreseeing the probable need of customs administration in those portions of the Philippine Archipelago that would have to be conquered as a result of the exigencies of the war, the President of the United States, acting under his authority as commander-in-chief of the Army and Navy, issued an order, under date of July 12, 1898, prescribing a tariff of duties and a schedule of taxes, previously prepared by the War Department, to be collected in the ports and places occupied by the forces of the United States in the Philippine Islands.[1]

By a tariff circular of the War Department on October 13, 1898, the operation of this order was suspended until the tenth day of the following November and the rates of the old Spanish tariff were enforced. The government thus recognized the wisdom of disturbing as little and changing as gradually as possible the conditions affecting trade and commerce. From time to time, however, in proportion as needed improvements essential to more efficient administration or the encouragement of Philippine-American trade re-

[1] *Customs Tariff and Regulations for the Philippine Islands*, Gov't Printing Office, Washington, 1899, p. 3.

lations revealed themselves, tariff circulars were issued by the War Department modifying either the schedules or regulations. When the Philippine Customs Tariff Act became effective on November 15, 1901, the last tariff circular, dated the same day, bore the designation, "Tariff Circular, No. 121." [1]

THE PHILIPPINE CUSTOMS TARIFF ACT OF NOVEMBER 15, 1901

In a letter sent the 20th day of April, 1899 to the President of the Chamber of Commerce of San Francisco, ten American commercial firms of Manila complained of the onerous duties American products had to bear under the modified Spanish tariff then in force. They urged a reduction of at least one-half of the rates upon articles of consumption, asked for a higher rate upon articles of luxury and a low tariff on productions special to the United States. They maintained that such changes would increase the customs revenues by a large percentage and would enable the United States to "derive some benefit accruing from the victories gained by her soldiers and sailors." They saw in those reductions the opening of a new field for American "fictile and textile manufacturers" and the agricultural products of the United States. With such reductions in rates to permit the Filipinos to bring in imports at as low a price as possible, they saw no objection to the granting of reciprocal privileges to all nations, for they were confident that "American goods could and would compete with productions from any country in the world." [2]

Other letters requesting revision came from business houses in America, which desired to extend their trade rela-

[1] *Customs Tariff and Regulations for the Philippine Islands*, Gov't Printing Office, Washington, 1899, p. 3.

[2] *S. Doc.* 171, 57th Cong., 1st Sess., p. 6.

tions to the Philippines and asked for the amendment of the tariff customs regulations in order to enable them to charge reasonable prices and still make a fair margin of profit.

The obvious need for revision prompted the War Department on the 22nd of May, 1900, to send a message to General MacArthur at Manila declaring tariff revision to be a matter of "vital importance," asking the Commanding General if he had officers qualified to form a board for tariff revision, and requesting his recommendation. To this message, the military governor replied that qualified officers were available and that the work should be done at Manila. The approval of the War Department having been secured previously, he appointed, on June 9, 1900, a Board of Officers to revise the United States provisional customs tariff and regulations for the Philippine Islands.[1]

The procedure of the Board is best described in the following extract from its report:

> To say that there is not a merchant or importer in Manila of respectable trade affiliations who has not been advised of the desire of the board to listen to all complaints and to receive all information that would tend to the improvement of the present system of tariff charges is believed to be a conservative statement, and it is felt that wherever the system of charges and imposts submitted with this report may, upon actual application or upon special and particular analysis of the different sections, prove unequal or inadequate, the apathy shown by the merchants and importers in the matters directly affecting their own interests will be largely to blame therefor.

On August 25, 1900, the report of the Army Board was turned over to the United States Philippine Commission, and by December 29th of the same year the commission had revised and transmitted the proposed act to the War De-

[1] *S. Doc.* 134, 57th Cong., 1st Sess., p. 4.

partment for approval. In the letter of transmittal, the Commissioners frankly admitted their inability to publish the bill in its entirety in the islands and the incomplete publication of only the first nine chapters in the newspapers there. "The intention of the Commission," said the commissioners, "that proposed legislation affecting the public should be published before action failed, therefore, of accomplishment as to this act." [1]

It was the intention of the Secretary of War to give full opportunity to business firms of the United States to present their comments on the proposed tariff before it became a law.[2] On its receipt by the War Department, five hundred copies were ordered printed and later distributed to newspapers, trade papers, boards of trade, commercial bodies, chambers of commerce, exporters, and manufacturers in all parts of the country for suggestion and recommendation.

A vast majority of the comments received took the form of technical discussion of the various schedules, judged from the standpoint of facilitating, as much as possible, the importation of American products when not inconsistent with keeping the essentials of a competitive market and the production of the maximum amount of revenue.[3] After these suggestions had been considered, the War Department made its revision of the Commission draft; and that revision, with the exception of a few minor changes suggested by the Philippine Commission, became the customs tariff law of the Philippine Islands. The formalities of enactment were gone through by the Philippine Commission on September 17, 1901, and the law became effective on the fifteenth day of the following November.

[1] *S. Doc.* 134, 57th Cong., 1st Sess., p. 6.

[2] Cablegram of October 13, 1900 to Taft, Manila, in *S. Doc.* 171, 57th Cong., 1st Sess., p. 3.

[3] *S. Doc.* 171, 57th Cong., 1st Sess., *passim*.

It would be of no profit to examine in detail the different schedules of the Act. The manner of enactment and the identity of the various influences that had a voice in the preparation of the law are of far greater consequence than the enacted result. Illuminating sidelights are revealed by the correspondence in connection with this tariff act. Under date of August 5, 1900, James J. Hooker, President of the Cincinnati Board of Trade and Bureau of Transportation, presented his suggestions on the subject of tariff revision to the Philippine Tariff Board, composed of army officers.[1] He enunciated three principles that should be controlling in the construction of the Philippine tariff. They were:

First. There should be enough revenue from customs duties to provide for the financial requirements of the general government, a free public school system, harbor improvements, and light-house service.

Second. All manufactured and agricultural products of the United States, excepting beer, etc., ought to be admitted, if not free, at the lowest possible rate of duty.

Third. Provision should be made for the free entry of all machinery required for the development of the agricultural, timber, and mineral resources of the islands.

Touching on foreign policy, Mr. Hooker advocated the open door only for those countries whose colonies in Asia and Africa were also open to American commerce. As a part of this program of foreign policy he would stimulate the importation of food products from Australia. "The vigorous and progressive Anglo-Saxons there," he said, "should be encouraged by every means to aid us in the Philippines."

An interesting fact in connection with the efforts by business firms to amend the Philippine Commission draft of the

[1] *S. Doc.* 171, 57th Cong., 1st Sess., p. 30.

tariff was the enlisting of, or the attempt to enlist, the services of members of Congress in influencing the final decision. The Keystone Watch Case Company, which took the lead among the watch manufacturers in the fight against the specific duty on watches with, it must be said, very strong arguments against the form of the proposed duty, sent a letter to Senator T. C. Platt of New York City on April 9, 1901.[1] Arguing for their suggested changes in the watch schedule, the representatives of the company declared the issue to be one of vast importance to the great watch industry of the United States, which was then progressing by leaps and bounds in the foreign markets of the world. The proposed schedule, it was asserted, would create havoc in the watch exporting industry. The Elgin Watch Company of Elgin, Illinois, they said, were with them in their fight for the change from the specific to the ad valorem form of duty. And concluding, the letter said:

> I wish, if it is possible, that you would look over as much of this correspondence as you can and let me know at once if you are in a position to help us any in this matter, and what you would advise us to do.
>
> Of course, Senator, this is nothing in any way connected with politics, but is a matter of business which the Keystone Watch Case Company would like to have your assistance in.

In connection with the difficulties encountered in classification in the cotton schedule, a statement by Tasker H. Bliss, then major in the army and collector of customs for Cuba, proved prophetic. He said, in a letter to the Secretary of War, dated at Habana, Cuba, April 9, 1901, that the amended cotton schedule of the Cuban tariff contained a possibility of throwing the trade in cotton goods into the hands of the English and Spanish manufacturers even more

[1] *S. Doc.* 171, 57th Cong., 1st Sess., p. 177.

than had been the case theretofore. If that should result it would be, the Major thought, merely additional evidence tending to prove that "those manufacturers who manufacture with direct reference to the tariff governing the market which they wish to enter will always have the advantage over those who do not so manufacture."

Lieutenant-Colonel Clarence R. Edwards, Chief of the Division of Insular Affairs at the time, sent Mr. Taft, then President of the Philippine Commission, a letter dated March 21, 1901, in which he said: [1]

> Naturally the cases of Cuba and the Philippines are entirely different. While the new tariff for the former . . . will be for the protection and furtherance of Cuban interests, and not for the benefit of the United States as against the interests of that island, the tariff for the Philippines will be based upon what is considered best for those islands as well as for this country.

In the memorandum [2] transmitted to the Senate by the Secretary of War concerning the enactment of the Philippine Commission's Tariff Act, a resumé is given of the nature of the response that the business interests of the country gave to the published schedules of the tariff. San Francisco was interested in lowering the duty on gasoline "to give a market for gasoline launches, stoves, and articles of like character." New York exporters of precious and semi-precious stones objected to the specific duty on their articles and contended for an ad valorem rate, which they deemed more equitable. The *New York Journal of Commerce* published an article assailing the iron schedule and pointing out the inequalities due to "a dogged adherence to specific rates." Similarly, objections were offered

[1] *S. Doc.* 171, 57th Cong., 1st Sess., pp. 284-286.

[2] *S. Doc.* 134, 57th Cong., 1st Sess.

to some paragraphs of the chemical schedule. A few industries asked for better treatment for their manufactured products. The cotton schedule provoked serious protests from both Eastern and Western manufacturers, and their arguments had considerable weight in the decisions arrived at by the War Department. Would-be exporters of printing paper asked for a lower duty on their goods on the ground that such importations into the Philippines "would be an important factor in the educational development of the islands." Reductions were urged for harness and harness-makers' wares. Manufacturers of watch cases and watch movements fought a winning fight for the substitution of ad valorem for specific rates of duty. The inequitable character of specific rates on watches was demonstrated as well as their menace to the American watch exporting industry. Typewriters were also hailed as a potent educational influence, and consequently deserving of a lower rate. The rate on meats and canned goods of all kinds awakened lively interest in the Middle West and on the Pacific coast. It was also advocated that "the duty on alcohol be made much higher, in order to prevent the importation of the same for the purpose of making a composite liquor out of the pure alcohol, to the detriment of the revenue and the liquor sold in the Archipelago."

It will be seen that the whole of the legislative power that gave rise to the Tariff Act of 1901 was exercised by representatives of the President; that American interests were given as great an opportunity to influence the final result as, if not a greater one than, that accorded to native economic interests.

THE CONGRESSIONAL TARIFF ACT FOR THE PHILIPPINES OF MARCH 8, 1902

Hardly had a month elapsed after the coming into effect of the Philippine Tariff Act of 1901 before the whole structure of Filipino-American tariff relations was rudely shaken by the decision of the Supreme Court in the Fourteen Diamond Rings case holding, in accord with the De Lima case previously decided, that the Philippines were not "foreign territory" within the meaning of such clauses in the tariff laws of the United States. The operation of the Dingley Tariff Act of 1897, whose rates had been enforced against products coming from the Philippine Islands, was thus stopped by judicial interpretation. If the Philippine Islands did not come within the term "foreign territory," manifestly the duties levied on goods coming from "foreign" countries could not apply to the products of the islands. The same judicial pronouncements also threw the Philippine Customs Tariff Act of 1901, passed by the Philippine Commission but without positive sanction by Congress, into the area of legal uncertainty. For, although it was admitted that Congress could impose duties on Philippine goods coming to the United States and American goods exported into the islands, it was by no means certain that any other governmental entity such as the Philippine Commission was actually invested with the same power. This, among other things, seemed to necessitate the passage of the Act "temporarily to provide revenue for the Philippine Islands and for other purposes" which became a law, after passage by Congress and the signature of the President, on March 8, 1902 and contained, as one of its sections, the same Philippine Customs Tariff Act which was enacted by the Philippine Commission in September, 1901. The causes that led to the enactment of this law of March 8, 1902, together with the questions of policy that were thereby decided at least temporarily, will be discussed in the chapter on goods exported from the Philippine Islands to the United States. That America's "open door" policy in China had an influence on her attitude toward the Philippine tariff is shown by the remarks of Senator Lodge, the chairman of the Senate Committee on the Philippines. During the bill's progress through the Senate, Mr. Lodge laid stress on the bearing of the proposed legislation on America's Far Eastern policy. He spoke of the "open door" in China and contended that America could not be its advocate for that country and at the same time refuse to apply it to the commerce of other nations with the Philippines. "The maintenance of a non-discriminating tariff upon all articles entering the Philippine Islands," he argued, was essential to American commercial interests in the Far East.[1]

THE PHILIPPINE CUSTOMS TARIFF ACT OF MARCH 3, 1905

On January 23, 1905 a bill[2] was introduced in the lower house of Congress to "revise and amend the tariff laws of the Philippine Archipelago." It was referred to the House Committee on Ways and Means, which, on the thirteenth of the following month, reported another bill[3] as a substitute. In reporting the bill favorably[4] the Committee referred to the preliminary work of investigation and revision done by a Commission of experts, the insular government of the Philippines, and the Bureau of Insular Affairs of the War Department. Various interests in the islands were consulted in the preparation of the first draft, which was

[1] *Cong. Record*, 57th Cong., 1st Sess., p. 823.

[2] H. R. 18195.

[3] H. R. 18965.

[4] *H. R. Report* no. 4600, 58th Cong., 3rd Sess.

then sent to the Secretary of War, who, as in the previous case, again consulted all those in the United States interested in Philippine trade. The House Committee changed very slightly the original draft of the bill, leaving unaltered the essential principles underlying the measure.

On the whole, this new legislation followed the main lines of policy laid down in the Customs Tariff Act of 1901 and the Revenue Act of March 8, 1902. They were all designed to raise enough revenue to meet the expenses of the insular government. They were further intended, in the words of the Committee on Ways and Means,[1] to "give the United States what benefits there are arising from classification of goods. There is no preference in rates given to goods coming from the United States for the reason that by the terms of the Treaty of Paris, Spain would have the right of a similar preference on goods imported from Spain to the Philippines until January, 1909."

Describing the changes in schedules, the Committee mentioned the reduction of the duties on manufactured tobacco by 50 per cent, slight increases for the rates on the finer qualities of shoes, a nominal ad valorem duty of 5 per cent on agricultural and other machinery used in the islands and produced in the United States, a decrease by one-half in the duties on gasoline, and a reduction by one-third in the rates on mirrors.

By a provision of the bill (paragraph 276), power to increase the duty on rice within certain limits was delegated to the Philippine Commission. Plainly, the intent was to make provision for meeting the problem involved in the raising of that principal food product of the islands. Every year great quantities of rice had, and still have to be imported to supply local consumption. Changes in conditions would have to be met by changes in legislation. That was the

[1] *H. Report* no. 4600, 58th Cong., 3rd Sess.

purpose of entrusting this power to the hands of the Philippine Commission. It was realized that no possible changes in the tariff schedules would actually stimulate the exportation of rice from the United States to the Philippines in view of the proximity of the islands to other rice-producing and exporting countries. There was also inserted a slight duty on mineral waters imported into the Philippine Islands to protect the Philippine mineral water industry from Japanese competition. Lastly, authority was given to the Philippine Commission to regulate or prohibit the importation of opium.[1]

THE AMENDMENT TO THE PHILIPPINE CUSTOMS TARIFF ACT OF MARCH 3, 1905, APPROVED FEBRUARY 26, 1906

The attempt to encourage the importation of American cotton manufactures to the Philippines through changes in the classifications in the cotton schedule of the tariff has already been alluded to.[2] Far from being realized, however, the expectations of the authors of the revision of the cotton schedule were completely nullified by the course of events. It was necessary, therefore, that the mistake should be corrected and a new Congressional enactment sought. This was the reason that lay behind the introduction of a bill[3] which was reported to the House by the Committee on Ways and Means on January 25, 1906. Speaking of Section I of the bill, which was its most important provision, the Committee in explaining its *raison d'être* quoted a letter sent by the Merchant's Association of New York.[4] So per-

[1] For the debate on this bill see *Cong. Record*, 58th Cong., 3rd Sess., pp. 2993, 2998, 3714.

[2] See *supra*, the paragraphs on Customs Tariff Law of 1901 and the Act of March 8, 1902.

[3] H. R. 13104. The record of the debate on this law can be found in *Cong. Record*, 59th Cong., 1st Sess., pp. 2391, 2718, 2835.

[4] *H. R. Report* no. 582, 59th Cong., 1st Sess.

fectly did the reasons advanced by the letter coincide with the opinions of the committee members that the letter itself was inserted in the report and used as the document that expressed fully the motive of the proposed legislation.

The letter, the arguments of which the Committee on Ways and Means thus made its own, was written by Mr. Theodore T. Dorman in his capacity as Secretary of the Philippine Tariff Committee of the Merchants' Association of New York, to Colonel Clarence R. Edwards, Chief of the Bureau of Insular Affairs. It was dated December 18, 1905 and extracts from its pertinent passages are as follows:[1]

As the Committee of the Merchants' Association of New York upon the Philippine cotton tariff, we have just received a copy of the cablegram transmitted to you by W. Morgan Shuster, collector of Customs for the Philippine Islands, in reply to your cablegram recently sent him, in which you transmitted to him a summary of the recommendations of proposed amendments to the schedules on cotton goods in the present tariff made by this committee and approved by the Merchants' Association of New York and by American manufacturers. In order that you may have the whole situation before you in a manner most convenient for your consideration, we summarize our recommendations, giving a statement of the reasons why each recommendation is made. . . .

The first recommendation made by this committee is an additional paragraph and note to class IV, Group 3, Rule B, which reads as follows:

"Textiles having a false selvage on either one or both sides, shall be considered as goods improved in condition, and shall be liable, as the textile, to the duties leviable thereon, plus an additional surtax of one hundred per centum. This provision applies to all cotton fabrics.

"Note.—By a false selvage shall be understood an edge

[1] *H. R. Report* no. 582, 59th Cong., 1st Sess.

obtained by cutting, ripping, tearing or otherwise splitting the textile in the direction of the warp."

This recommendation of the Committee looks mainly to the establishment of a fair basis for introduction in the Philippine market of the American textiles woven with true selvages in all widths, but mainly in narrow widths, for example 25 inches. This recommendation is essential to the American manufacturers, as will appear from the following statement concerning the comparative situation as regards the manufacture of these fabrics in this country and abroad. Generally speaking, under any conditions of manufacture, the fabric is woven and run in a continuous piece through the different finishing processes as desired, namely sizing, bleaching, printing, dyeing, and calendering, and finally cut in pieces of convenient length, rolled or folded, packed in cases or bales and marketed.

In American mills there is a vast equipment of looms, printing and finishing machinery, designed to operate on textiles of narrow widths, and since designed for narrow widths these machines will not accommodate textiles of greater widths.

Among the European manufacturers a method designed to reduce the cost of manufacture is in practice as follows: Instead of originally weaving the textile in the width finally desired a special loom of double the width of the desired textile is used—that is, for a desired print of 25 inches width a loom of 52 inches is taken (2 inches being allowed for shrinkage in width during the finishing operations). At the center of this wide 52-inch textile two sets of heavy warp threads, slightly separated, are placed, and the fabric is woven 52 inches wide. Still, in this width, it is run through specially wide bleaching, printing, and finishing apparatus, and, as an additional operation after the completion of manufacturing and finishing, is split or torn lengthwise at the weak center line, between the two sets of heavy threads, giving two lengths of textiles of the original length woven, but only 25 inches wide. This additional operation gives to these textiles the name of "splits", and they can always be distinguished from goods manufactured in single widths with true selvage on each edge by the appearance of the false or "split selvage" along one of the sides.

Continuing, the Committee of the Merchants' Association said:

For the American manufacturers the European so-called "split" method of construction is at present economically and practically impossible. The present American equipment of narrow looms, printing and finishing machines would have to be supplanted by similar machines of wider construction. This would mean almost a complete loss of the present capital invested in textile machinery and an immense investment of new capital in wide machinery for this special purpose. More careful and skillful operators would have to be employed, as it requires greater care economically to run the wider machinery. This in turn would mean higher wages, and the American wage is already much higher than among European textile manufacturers. With the present automatic machinery a loom stops upon the breaking of a thread until the operator repairs the break and restarts the loom. For every minute that a wide loom stands idle the loss in production is double as compared with the loss on a narrow loom in the same situation, and with operators inexperienced in the use of wide machinery the loss would be proportionately greater.

And concluding, the letter set forth that:

. . . to place American goods of this character in the Philippine market upon a fair basis of competition with the "split" goods of European production, it is absolutely essential that approximate provisions, favorable to the American manufacturers, should be embodied in the Philippine tariff,

and that

. . . the needs and requirements of the American manufacturer should be considered primarily and fundamentally in any tariff imposed upon American goods going into the Philippine market.

In their approval of principles upon which these suggestions were based, their authors told of how they had refrained from offering amendments and requesting changes which from their knowledge and experience did not seem absolutely necessary and essential. They had also taken into account, so they asserted, the necessity of maintaining the revenues of the islands.

Mr. Payne, the Chairman of the Committee on Ways and Means, explained the necessity for action in the course of the debate in the House. He said that the proposed law was an attempt to revise and amend the customs tariff law for the Philippine Islands, which was passed on March 3, 1905. At that time a general revision was made of the tariff upon goods coming from the United States and foreign countries into the Philippines. An amendment of the cotton schedule was, at the time, inserted into the bill on the representations of a few men who claimed to represent the cotton manufacturers of the United States. The Committee on Ways and Means approved the amendment to the bill on the understanding that such a provision would work to the advantage of the American manufacturers. Mr. Payne then told how, later, it was discovered that the revised cotton schedule of 1905, far from facilitating the export of American cotton goods into the Philippines, had virtually excluded the sale of such goods in that market, the reason being the same one that was advanced by the Philippine Committee of the Merchants' Association of New York.[1]

[1] For Mr. Payne's remarks, see *Cong. Record*, 59th Cong., 1st Sess., pp. 2391 *et seq.*

The other minor changes that the bill proposed were decreases in some parts of the shoe schedule and the elimination of the export duty on cocoanuts. So cogent did the reasoning in favor of the bill seem to the Representatives and Senators that this proposed law was unanimously reported by the House Committee on Ways and Means, passed by the House itself, without a division, favorably reported to the Senate, again by a unanimous vote of its Committee on the Philippines, and approved by the Senators also, without a division. It was signed by the President and became a law on the 26th of February, 1906.

THE ACT OF AUGUST 5, 1909 TO "REVISE AND AMEND THE TARIFF LAWS OF THE PHILIPPINE ISLANDS"

Efforts to obtain free trade between America and the Philippines had been going on since the earliest period of the American régime and bills had been periodically introduced into Congress for such a purpose. It was not until 1909, however, that the proponents of free trade were able to wrest concessions from the opposing sugar and tobacco interests in the form of qualified free trade between the two countries under the general tariff law passed in that year. The enactment of the Payne-Aldrich tariff law, with provisions for limited free trade between America and the Philippines, it was thought would create a gap of about a million dollars in Philippine customs revenues,[1] which it was necessary to fill from some other source. In addition, it was deemed desirable to have the customs tariff regulations in the islands conform, as nearly as possible, to those of the United States, especially with respect to packing and packages. These things made necessary the passage of a separate law to amend the tariff laws of the Philippines.

[1] *H. R. Report* no. 7, 61st Cong., 1st Sess.

The draft of the bill was drawn by a Board of Tariff experts in Manila, headed by the insular collector of customs. Extensive public hearings were held and the schedules agreed upon were submitted to the Bureau of Insular Affairs, which revised them after having them published throughout the country for suggestions and criticism. The chief of the Bureau gave it as his belief that the draft had reconciled the contending interests and that the schedules would, on that account, not encounter opposition.[1]

The bill was introduced in the House on March 3, 1909, and passed by that body on the 24th of the same month. Favorable action was had in the Senate on July 9th and, with the signature of the President, the bill became law on August 5, 1909.

Mr. Payne, Chairman of the House Committee on Ways and Means, explained in the course of the debate the nature of the amendment that his committee made on the schedules that had been submitted by the Bureau of Insular Affairs of the War Department.[2] Most of the changes he declared to be merely in the phraseology of the bill although there were a few alterations that represented material modifications in schedules. Two of these changes were the removal of the proposed duty on petroleum or any of its products and the lowering of the proposed schedule rates for rails of light weight and sugar machinery. Just how this discriminating duty on light weight rails and sugar machinery came to be included in the draft prepared by the Philippine Tariff Board and the Bureau of Insular Affairs was frankly discussed by Mr. Payne in the speech already alluded to. The general duties on the other items in the iron schedule he placed at 15 per cent ad valorem. Light weight rails and

[1] *H. R. Doc.* 14, 61st Cong., 1st Sess.

[2] See his remarks in *Cong. Record*, 61st Cong., 1st Seess., pp. 1998 *et seq.*

sugar machinery had to bear the burden of a 30 per cent ad valorem duty. Those rails belonged to the kind used in building tramways or railroads for sugar plantations. Manifestly the authorship of this discriminating duty on these light rails could be sought for in those places that did not harbor wishes for the expansion of the Philippine sugar industry. This investigation, Mr. Payne said, the Committee made, and its members came across a supposed ultimatum by certain manufacturers giving the framers of the measure a choice between either an insertion of the desired discrimination or attendance upon the funeral ceremonies of their legislative infant. It is but fair to add that Mr. Payne disclaimed absolute knowledge of either the truth or falsity of the information he and his committee members had unearthed. Be it said, also, that the Chairman and members of the Committee on Ways and Means proved themselves men of mettle, erased the discriminating duty, and successfully piloted the measure through the seas of legislative uncertainty.

Two other provisions of the law worthy of mention were the items extending protection to the manufacture of matches and of bolts and nuts for structural steel, which were infant industries of the Philippines. Taken all in all, however, the policy underlying this Philippine Tariff Revision Law of August 5, 1909, as was the case with the preceding ones (for there was not any new departure of policy, at this time, as far as the customs tariff was concerned) was the extension of American trade.[1]

[1] For the Congressional debates on this law of August 5, 1909, H. R. 9135, see *Cong. Record*, 61st Cong., 1st Sess., pp. 1997-2012, 2119-2125, 2126, 2237, 2338, 4326, 4338, 5086.

THE TARIFF ACT OF 1913 AND THE PHILIPPINE CUSTOMS TARIFF

The passage of the Underwood Tariff Law of 1913 did not at all affect the then existing status of customs duties on goods imported into the Philippines from the United States and other countries. The Act of August 5, 1909 was changed only in that section providing for export duties on certain Philippine products sent to countries, other than the United States, which duties were repealed by paragraph C of section IV of this Tariff Act of 1913.

This Underwood Tariff Law of 1913, in its provisions relating to the Philippine customs tariff, completes the list of Congressional legislation on the subject of the duties on goods imported into the Philippine Islands. In 1901 the Philippine Commission, deriving its authority from the power granted to the President of the United States, passed a customs tariff act designed to produce adequate revenues and encourage American trade; in 1902 the decision in the insular cases, handed down in the latter part of 1901, made it seem desirable for Congress to clothe with its legislative authority what had previously been only a statute of the Philippine Commission; in 1905 a general revision was undertaken along the lines of the act of 1901 but with pronounced changes in the cotton schedule intended to benefit American manufacturers;[1] in 1906 the cotton schedule was again amended, for experience had shown the futile results of the changes in the preceding year; in 1909 another tariff revision was made necessary by the establishment of limited free trade and an attempt to include discriminating duties on rails and machinery used in sugar production met with defeat at the hands of the House Committee on Ways and Means; in 1913 the Underwood tariff abolished the export

[1] *Supra*, p. 74.

duties on Philippine products and removed the limitations on the quantity to be admitted free of duty.

Throughout that series of laws determining the duties to be paid on products imported into the islands runs the thread of that policy of the enjoyment of economic benefits, if that could be done without the exploitation of the colonial dependency. Obviously, the application of such a principle depends upon the interpretation of what is or is not embraced in the term "exploitation". It may be taken as on the whole true that, in the laws thus far examined, the considerations that entered into their enactment apparently were:

First, the raising of sufficient income for the carrying out of America's Philippine policy, *i. e.,* to meet the financial needs of the sort of local government that she was disposed to set up in accordance with her evolving policies, however temporary or uncertain they may have been.

Second, the facilitating of American exports and consumption of American goods whenever such did not involve too drastic discrimination.[1]

Third, regard for the welfare of the natives.

The Export Duties on Philippine Products

An interesting phase of Philippine-American economic relations has been the existence and the effect on trade between the two countries of the export duties collected from the four principal exports in the years of 1898-1913. These export taxes had been one of the sources of revenue during the Spanish régime. A schedule of duties, similar to those during Spanish times, was incorporated in the Provisional

[1] For a discussion of the discriminatory provisions of the early tariff acts levying duties on goods imported into the Philippines, seee Willis, *Our Philippine Problem*, ch. xii. On the subject of America's economic policy, see the suggestive speech of Congressman Hill in *Cong. Record*, 61st Cong., 1st Sess., pp. 2010 *et seq.*

Customs Tariff of 1898.[1] Section 13 of the Customs Tariff Act [2] approved by the Philippine Commission also contained similar provisions.

THE PHILIPPINE TARIFF ACT OF MARCH 8, 1902

When the time came for Congress to consider tariff legislation for the Philippines, one of the sections of the Act "temporarily to provide revenue for the Philippine Islands and for other purposes" [3] provided, among other things, for the deduction of the export taxes from the tariff duties on Philippine products when sent to the United States and the exemption of those Philippine articles on the free list in the United States tariff from the payment of export duties when exported directly to, and for use and consumption in, the United States. The last clause was designed to relieve hemp which was on the free list in the United States tariff from paying an export tax in the Philippines when shipped to the United States.

It was felt by the members of Congress, at least by the Chairman of the Senate Committee on the Philippines, that if Philippine sugar and tobacco were granted reductions in tariff duties equivalent to the export dues paid in the islands, hemp, which was on the free list, should also be freed from the export taxes when imported into the United States. The same gentleman (the Chairman of the Senate Committee) thought the change to be, beyond doubt, to the advantage of the hemp growers of the Philippine Islands. And, in his estimation, it was "equally beyond question" that it would be "to the advantage of the people of the United States." [4]

[1] See secs. 297-307 of the Customs Tariff Schedules in *Customs Tariff and Regulations for the P. I.*, 1899.

[2] See the Tariff Act of Nov. 15, 1901.

[3] See sec. 2, *Public*, no. 28, 32 *U. S. Statutes*, 54.

[4] See Speech of Senator Lodge, *Cong. Record*, 57 Cong., 1st Sess., pp. 822 *et seq*.

What the United States Philippine Commission thought of this section of the Tariff Act is shown in one of its annual reports.[1] There the Commission declared it desired to "call attention to the injustice effected upon the revenues of the Islands. . . ." The Commission reported that under the operation of that section the Philippine government had, up to the close of the fiscal year 1904, collected $1,060,-460.20 in import duties which were refundable. Most of these refundable duties were on hemp exportations. Concluding, the Commission said: "No good reason is perceived why this bounty to American manufacturers should be extracted from the treasury of the Philippine Islands, and it is respectfully submitted that the law authorizing it should be repealed."

PROVISIONS REGARDING THE EXPORT TAX IN SUCCEEDING TARIFF LAWS UP TO 1909

In the Philippine Tariff Act of March 3, 1905,[2] the export tax provisions were found in paragraphs 398-406 of Section 13. While there were slight changes in phraseology, there was no substantial alteration in any of the items. On the 26th of February, 1906, came another Tariff Act to amend the Tariff Act of the previous year.[3] This time the only change was the removal of the export duty on cocoanuts.

THE EXPORT TAX IN THE PHILIPPINE CUSTOMS TARIFF ACT OF 1909

Section 13 of the Philippine Tariff Act of August 5, 1909, did not change the then existing provisions regarding

[1] See *Report of the Phil. Commission*, Nov., 1904, pp. 26 *et seq.*

[2] See *Public*, no. 141, *U. S. Statutes*, 975.

[3] *Public*, no. 27, 34 *U. S. Statutes*, 24.

export duties.[1] However, it produced a discussion which, though cursory and of but a few minutes' duration, was much more extended than those that had arisen previously since the Tariff Act of 1902 was approved.

Mr. Payne, in fathering the measure, remarked that the insertion of the exemption of Philippine products from the export tax when sent to the United States in the Act of 1902 had worked a " revolution commercially in regard to hemp." Before the passage of the law of 1902 most of the hemp production of the Philippines had gone to countries other than the United States. A few years after the Act had gone into effect, the United States was importing over half of the hemp exports of the islands. Mr. Payne admitted that the tax was foreign to the Constitution and the American system of government, but held it to be justified in the Philippines on the ground that conditions there were different. He claimed the tax to be really a tax on land or the produce of the land.[2]

On the other hand, Representative Underwood strongly opposed the proposed continuation of the tax in respect of exports to any foreign country and condemned it in scathing terms. He objected to it because it was not " justified by any economic principle of government." He declared it to be a tax which had been abandoned by practically all of the civilized nations, because it bore heavily on the ability

[1] See paragraph 325-355 of Sec. 13, *Public*, no. 7, 36 *U. S. Statutes* 174. Mention is also made of Philippine export duties in Section 5 of the U. S. Tariff Act of Aug. 5, 1909, *Public*, no. 5, 36 *U. S. Statutes* 84.

[2] *Cong. Record*, 61st Cong., 1st Sess., pp. 1999, 2121. Professor Willis and Judge Blount are in agreement in holding that the exemption of hemp exported to the U. S. from the export tax operated solely for the benefit of the cordage manufacturers. See Willis, *Our Philippine Problem* (New York, 1905), pp. 283-284, and Blount, *The American Occupation of the Philippines* (New York, 1912), ch. 26.

of one nation to compete with the other nations in foreign markets.[1] It may be added that, due to the political complexion of the 61st Congress, this objection from the leader of the Democrats did not prevent the passage of the bill.

THE U. S TARIFF ACT OF OCTOBER 3, 1913

The political overturn of 1912 resulted in the placing of Mr. Underwood and his associates in a position to dictate legislation. In view of his previous utterances on the export tax it was to be expected that he would work for its repeal. Section IV of the U. S. Tariff Act of 1913[2] dealt with tariff relations between the Philippines and the United States and its last proviso expressly repealed the export tax section of the Philippine Customs Tariff Act of April 5, 1909, thus removing all taxes that had theretofore been imposed on Philippine exports to foreign countries other than the United States. Section 11 of the Philippine Autonomy Act of 1916 forbids the imposition of any tax on exports by the Philippine Legislature.

[1] *Cong. Record*, 61st Cong., 1st Sess., pp. 2008 *et seq.*

[2] *Public*, no. 16, 38 *U. S. Statutes* 113.

CHAPTER V

TARIFF ON PHILIPPINE GOODS EXPORTED TO THE UNITED STATES

THE PHILIPPINE TARIFF ACT OF MARCH 8, 1902

THE Philippine Customs tariff act, enacted by the Philippine Commission and fixing the import duties on goods entering the islands, had been based on the war power of the President and the blanket authority that had been granted him by the Spooner amendment.[1] The schedule of duties contained in this customs tariff law of 1901 applied alike to products of the United States and those of other countries entering the Philippines. Such non-discrimination in regard to tariff rates was due to the fact that, under the Treaty of Paris, Spanish products, during the first ten years after the ratification of peace, were entitled to equal treatment with those of the United States.[2] Doubts were entertained, in connection with this treaty right of Spain, as to whether, under the most-favored-nation clause of America's commercial agreements with the other powers, the United States would not be forced to grant to those countries the same privileges as were given to Spain. Of course, a general reduction of duties applicable to the products of all countries would not have been in violation of the treaty's stipulation. But that would have meant the disappearance of the main source of revenue for the islands and the erec-

[1] See the Army Appropriation Act of Mar. 2, 1901, 31 *U. S. Stat. L.*, 895.

[2] Act IV of the Treaty.

tion of a barrier to the successful execution of America's task of governing them.

Congressional enactment of a tariff act for the Philippines was made imperative by the decision of the United States Supreme Court in the diamond rings case in 1901. On December 13, of that year, the Committee on Ways and Means of the House of Representatives favorably reported a bill [1] entitled "An Act temporarily to provide revenue for the Philippine Islands and for other purposes" containing provisions for:

1. The levying of the rates of the Dingley tariff law on Philippine products. These rates were later reduced 25 per cent by a Senate amendment.

2. The enactment of the Philippine Customs Tariff Act of the Philippine Commission as a part of the statutes of the United States.

3. The collection of tonnage taxes on vessels plying between the ports of the United States and the Philippines.

4. Dealing with the questions of the United States internal-revenue tax on American goods exported to the islands, the duties paid upon foreign goods imported to the United States and used in the manufacture of articles sent to the Philippines, and the application of the coastwise law to the bottoms engaged in Philippine-American trade.

Obviously, there were two possible paths of policy open to Congress after the Supreme Court's decision. It could have chosen the path of free trade, qualified or unqualified, between the two countries. Or it could have re-established by further legislation, under the admitted power of Congress so to do, the conditions prevailing during the automatic application of the Dingley tariff law until they were disturbed by the scruples of the judicial conscience. What

[1] H. R. 5833.

course the gentlemen of the Congress followed is a matter of history and of record; what reasons swayed and determined the Congressional mind are matters for investigation and of opinion.

In favorably reporting the bill under consideration, (H. R. 5833) the Senate Committee on the Philippines referred to the decision of the Supreme Court as the cause for the "pressing emergency" which the bill was designed to meet. And the intent of the bill, the Committee said, was the restoration of the status preceding the Court's decision.[1]

Demolition of the tariff barrier on Philippine products through judicial interpretation thus, in the minds of Congressmen, gave rise to a "pressing emergency." Was it because of the loss of the duties collected in American ports on Philippine products—duties which were turned over to the Philippine government? The revenue loss would assuredly have been considerable but that could hardly have been termed a "pressing emergency." Much more serious would have been the possibility that the Supreme Court's decision might be interpreted to include, possibly, the customs duties levied on goods entering the Philippines. However, that was at best nothing more than a legal possibility—one of so uncertain a nature as not to warrant being termed the main cause of the "pressing emergency" that so suddenly impressed the House Committee on Ways and Means, the Senate Committee on the Philippines, and a majority of the Representatives and Senators at Washington.

On the floor of the Senate, this question of the real policy prompting the passage of the law naturally stirred considerable discussion. Senator Rawlins, in opposing the bill, gave it as his opinon that the revenue argument could not stand

[1] *S. Doc.* 181, 57th Cong., 1st Sess.

the test of actual facts. He quoted official reports and statements of the Chairman of the Committee on the Philippines to show that the revenue loss would not seriously embarass the finances of the Philippine government. He asserted that the real question was whether the Islands should be treated as American territory and their inhabitants placed on the same footing as American citizens. "The Supreme Court", he said, "having decided that in the normal operations of government there should be free trade between the islands and the people of the United States, this bill is an urgent bill for the purpose of precluding the possibility of that."[1] Authoritative corroboration of the correctness of Senator Rawlins' line of thought in this particular instance was supplied by the remarks of the Chairman of the House Committee in charge of the bill.[2] To him the possibility of the importation of Philippine products into the United States free of duty constituted the "pressing emergency." He stated that the prompt passage of the bill by the House had operated to frustrate the plans for the formation of a syndicate of American capitalists to bring in cargoes of tobacco from the islands.

After the favorable report by the Committee on Ways and Means to the House of Representatives on December 13, 1901, debate was had on the bill nearly a week later. Louisiana spoke through Representative Robertson who expressed his determination never to vote for free sugar or any bill proposing it; and he voiced the conviction that the passage of the bill was "best for his constituents" and its failure would be "disastrous to the sugar interests of Louisiana in the future." Pennsylvania, also, ran true to form. One of her representatives, Mr. Dalzell, found the

[1] For Senator Rawlins' Speech, see *Cong. Record*, 57th Cong., 1st Sess., p. 1061.

[2] *Cong. Record*, 57th Cong., 1st Sess., p. 2189.

strongest argument for the bill in the philippic delivered against it by Mr. Swanson, of Virginia, who saw in the bill the creation of advantages to American producers "in the Philippine markets" and the protection of American labor in her own markets against "the cheap labor of the Philippines." Mr. Swanson's speech, to which Mr. Dalzell made reference, contained the most exhaustive comparison of the schedules of the proposed tariff in this country and in the Philippines on the commerce between the two countries. The bill contained schedules of duties in American and foreign goods when imported into the Philippines and a different schedule of dues to be paid by products of the Philippine Islands when imported into the United States. The representative from Virginia showed how, under the parallel schedules of the bill, tobacco produced in the United States could enter the islands on payment of a duty of 22 cents per pound, while Philippine tobacco had to pay a duty of $1.85 per pound with a heavy export tax in addition; American cigars had to pay only 88 cents per pound, while Philippine cigars, entering the United States, paid a duty of $4.50 per pound, an ad valorem duty of 25 per cent, and, also, an export duty; he cited the case of sugar and compared the duty of $17 per ton on that commodity exported either from the United States, Porto Rico or Hawaii with the $36 duty per ton on Philippine sugar with an export tax in addition; he mentioned the case of iron ore where a 25-cent duty on one side contrasted with a 67-cent duty on the other. He concluded that the rates of duty on Philippine products sent to the United States were "heavy, exorbitant, restrictive." They were such, he said, as could give "no encouragement to enterprise" and "no development to trade and commerce." [1]

[1] For the speeches of Representatives Robertson, Dalzell and Swanson, see *Cong. Record*, 57th Cong., 1st Sess., pp. 322-3. 368, 425.

The fight for a reduction of the duties on Philippine products was strongly pressed by the Philippine Commission, the Bureau of Insular Affairs of the War Department, and the President of the United States during this and the immediately succeeding years. In the opinion of Mr. Taft, the governor of the Philippines, a reduction of at least 50 per cent was required to obtain appreciable economic benefits for the islands, with the consequent moral effect favorable to pacification. In fact, this political aspect of the reduction of the rates was uppermost in his mind.[1] That Mr. Taft was conservative when he asked for a 50 per cent reduction in the Dingley rates is shown by the cablegrams exchanged betwen him and Vice-Governor Wright whom he had left as Acting Governor at Manila. Replying to Mr. Taft's cabled inquiry as to the probable effect of a 50 per cent reduction, Governor Wright answered that public hearings in Manila had considered the question and discovered a sentiment strongly favoring a 75 per cent reduction on the ground that one of only 50 per cent would leave the tariff almost prohibitive. The acting Governor thought the bigger reduction would be a measure of relief and would produce an excellent political effect.[2]

However, in spite of Mr. Taft's staunch advocacy of the Philippine side of the debate he, in the course of the hearings conducted by the Senate Committee on the Philippines, clearly defined his position in the answer he gave to one of Senator Patterson's questions. Asked whether he would "knowingly advocate any policy that would injure the industries of the United States—his own country," the then governor of the Philippines said: "I do not think I would. We do not approach it from the standpoint of those interests, however."

[1] *S. Doc.* 331, 57th Cong., 1st Sess., pp. 159, 165.

[2] *S. Doc.* 331, 57th Cong., 1st Sess.

The moral effect of such economic concessions to the Islands, Senator Mitchell emphasized on the floor of the Senate.[1] He would give concessions that would instill encouragement, confidence and hope among the Filipinos; he would hold up before them the wide difference between the "iron and hurtful rule of the Spaniard and the beneficent and helpful rule of the American," business prospects which would turn their minds "from the attractions of the arts of war to those of the arts of peace."

Such were the varied considerations that resulted in the Congressional act of March 8, 1902 "temporarily to provide revenue for the Philippine Islands, etc." Removal of the duties on Philippine products through the non-application of the Dingley rates on imports from foreign countries produced a state of things that alarmed not a few protectionists. They asked for protection against the prostrate condition of Philippine industries, at the time, and more particularly their potential future. On the other hand, native economic interests in the Philippines clamored for a reduction of at least 75 per cent in the Dingley rates to give them the benefit of the American market. The representatives of the American government in the Philippines and administration officials at Washington, concerned with the affairs of the Philippine government, supported the request for reduction on the ground that it would have been a benefit to Philippine industries, without being a detriment to American interests, and an effective factor in the solution of the problems facing American administrators in the Philippines. The issue was thus joined. Congress decided. It determined the tariff on American goods exported to the Philippines and the duties to be levied on Philippine products entering the United States. It provided on the Philippine end of the line a tariff for revenue; at the

[1] For his speech see *Cong. Record*, 57th Cong., 1st Sess., p. 1690.

American end it raised anew the standard of protectionism, granting to Philippine producers and exporters a reduction of only 25 per cent from the Dingley rates.[1]

THE STRUGGLE FOR THE REDUCTION OF RATES ON PHILIPPINE PRODUCTS EXPORTED TO THE U. S.

In the course of the year following the passage of the act of March 8, 1902, the question of the reduction of the tariff on Philippine products acquired the nature of an emergency measure. It was urged in order to relieve in a constructive way the universal economic distress in the Philippine Archipelago. The islands had been the scene of continuously devastating warfare for almost six years and there had been superimposed on that unsettlement of social conditions and habits of industry and order the loss of 90 per cent of their principal work animals through rinderpest, and three quarters of their rice crop—which constituted and still constitutes their principal article of diet. So serious did the government deem the situation to be that on February 27, 1903, the President sent a special message to the Senate which, at the time, had under consideration the bill, already passed by the House, for tariff reduction on Philippine products. The message was as follows:[2]

WHITE HOUSE, FEB. 27, 1903.

TO THE SENATE:

I have just received a cable from Governor Taft which runs as follows:

" Necessity for passage House tariff bill most urgent. The conditions of productive industry and business considerably

[1] For the debates on this law see *Cong. Record*, 57th Cong., 1st Sess., pp. 328, 409, 425, 822, 866, 813, 993, 1002, 1056, 1084, 1115, 1166, 1228, 1326, 1348, 1387, 1437, 1441, 1442, 1498, 1574, 1640, 1680, 1682, 1736, 1849, 1800, 1956, 2015, 2075, 2090, 2092, 2103.

[2] *Messages and Papers of the Presidents*, vol. xv, p. 6737.

worse than in November, the date of last report, and growing worse each month. Some revival in sugar, tobacco prices due to expectation of tariff law. The interest of Filipinos in sugar and tobacco extensive, and failure of bill will be blow in face of those interests. Number of tobacco factories will have to close, and many sugar haciendas will be put up for sale at a sacrifice, if the bill will not pass. Customs receipts have fallen off this month one-third, showing decrease of purchasing power of islands. General business stagnant. All political parties, including labor unions, most strenuous in petition for tariff bill. Effect of its failure very discouraging."

Vice-Governor Luke Wright indorses in the strongest manner all that Governor Taft has said, and states that he has the gravest apprehension as to the damage that may come to the islands if there is not a substantial reduction in the tariff levied against Philippine goods coming into the U. S. I very earnestly ask that this matter receive the immediate attention of Congress and that the relief prayed for be granted.

As Congress knows, a series of calamities have befallen the Philippine people. Just as they were emerging from nearly six years of devastating warfare, with the accompanying destruction of property and the breaking up of the bonds of social order and the habits of peaceful industry, there occurred an epidemic of rinderpest which destroyed 90 per cent of the carabaos, the Filipino cattle, leaving the people without draft animals to till the land or to aid in the ordinary work of farm and village life. The extent of the disaster can be seen from the fact that the surviving carabaos have increased over tenfold in value. At the same time a peculiar oriental horse disease became epidemic, further crippling transportation. The rice crop, already reduced by various causes to but a fourth of its ordinary size, has been damaged by locusts, so that the price of rice has nearly doubled.

Under these circumstances there is imminent danger of famine in the islands. Congress is in course of generously appropriating $3,000,000 to meet the immediate needs; but the indispensable and preëminent need is the resurrection of productive industry from the prostration into which it has been thrown by the causes above enumerated. I ask action in the tariff matter, not merely from the standpoint of wise governmental policy, but as a measure of humanity in response to an appeal to which this great people should not close its ears. We have assumed responsibility toward the Philippine Islands which we are in honor bound to fulfil. We have the specific duty of taking every measure in our power to see to their prosperity. The first and most important step in this direction has been accomplishment by the joint action of the military and civil authorities in securing peace and civil government. The wisdom of Congress at the present session has provided for them a stable currency and its spirit of humane liberality and justice toward them will be shown in the appropriation now substantially agreed upon of $3,000,000 to meet the pressing, immediate necessities; but there remains a vital need that one thing further shall be done. The calamities which have befallen them as above enumerated could have been averted by no human wisdom. They cannot be completely repaired; but the suffering can be greatly alleviated and a permanent basis of future prosperity assured if the economic relations of the islands with the United States are put upon a satisfactory basis.

THE COOPER BILL FOR REDUCTION—H. R. 15702—DEC. 5, 1902

The bill[1] before the Senate, which was the subject of the special message of President Roosevelt, was introduced in the House by Representative Cooper on Decembr 5, 1902. To back its favorable report on the bill, the House Committee on Ways and Means quoted from the War Department report for 1902 in an effort to picture the same serious situation that the President had depicted in his special mes-

[1] H. R. 15702.

sage. Faced with this situation, the Senate Committee on the Philippines favorably reported, with two amendments, the House bill which had passed that chamber on December 17, 1902.[1] One of these two amendments provided for the free admission to the Philippine Islands during five years of all material to be used in the construction or equipment of railroads. The other and more important one granted a reduction of the duties on Philippine sugar and tobacco entering the United States not to 25 per cent of the Dingley rates, as was the case in the House bill, but to 50 per cent.

The chairman of the Committee, Mr. Lodge, replying to Senator Foraker's argument for the original House provision[2] confessed his preference for the larger reduction, but was willing to take the bill with a smaller reduction rather than lose it for that session, at any rate, by insisting on the original reduction. Later on, he said:[3]

> In the vast volume of the imports of the United States the small amount of the increase in sugar and tobacco that would come by the passage of this bill would go unnoticed. But, small as it is to us, it may mean life or death to hundreds of those people. We have given them $3,000,000 in the sundry civil appropriation bill to restock their farms and help them buy cattle and start again; but the greatest charity, the largest humanity, that we can show to them is to open the channels for reviving business.

As the debate progressed certain sidelights gradually were unfolded. One of the opponents of the bill was Senator Patterson, of Colorado, a Democrat and vehement anti-

[1] For the Reports of the House and Senate Committees, see *H. R. Report* no. 2907, and *S. Report* no. 2586, 57th Cong., 2nd Sess.

[2] *Cong. Record*, 57th Cong., 2nd Sess., p. 2186.

[3] *Ibid.*, p. 2978.

imperialist. He reasoned out that there being little or no conflict between the products of the Philippines and those of the New England and Middle West states, it was understandable why the Senators from those states were quite willing to have absolute free trade between the Philippines and the United States.[1] As for himself, Senator Patterson announced that he represented one state "surrounded by other states that were deeply interested in the item of sugar, and until there was revision of the tariff that would take into view every item upon it, making an equitable reduction all along the line," he would oppose "interfering in any degree with the duties upon the particular industry" he was defending.

Senator Bacon of Georgia favored the bill as an act of justice to the Philippines in spite of the fact that his state produced tobacco. He did not, however, believe there would be any dumping of Philippine products as a result of the legislation he was in favor of. Another Senator (Senator Carmack of Tennessee) declared his intention of voting for "correct and honest principles of government." He would not,—he went on,—desert those principles in order to favor men in his state or anywhere else. Concerning the interesting question of why the Senate Committee on the Philippines agreed to the amendment of the House provision, the Tennessee Senator referred to, what he termed, the "notorious" fact of the change having been due to the opposition of the President of the American Beet Sugar Association.[2]

In spite of such powerful appeals from the responsible

[1] *Cong. Record*, 57th Cong., 2nd Sess., p. 2979.

[2] *Cong. Record*, 57th Cong., 2nd Sess., p. 2991; see also pamphlet of the American Beet Sugar Association issued Dec. 29, 1904 and printed in the appendix of the *Hearings on the Philippine Tariff* before the Committee on Ways and Means, 59th Cong., 1st Sess.

authorities handling the situation in the islands, the Senate failed to pass the bill before that session of Congress ended. The embattled Senators who were apprehensive of the future of the sugar industry won. The senior Senator from Massachusetts (Senator Hoar) pronounced the epilogue. "Here are nine or ten million people," he said, "upon whom is impending a terrible famine accompanied by pestilence. This does not rest on the authority of discontent. The statement comes from the Philippine people through their chieftain, Aguinaldo, and in even more terrible language from Governor Taft. If nine or ten million Americans had such a calamity impending over them, we would lay aside every thought of other business or affairs; we would have an extra session of Congress; we would sit day and night; the whole resources of the charity and the wealth and the humanity of the American people would be taxed to their utmost."[1]

THE CURTIS BILL H. R. 17752 OF JANUARY 14, 1905

The next effort of any considerable importance to secure a reduction of the tariff rates on Philippine products was the one represented by the Curtis bill introduced in the House on the 14th of January, 1905. Its importance consisted not so much in its prospects of being converted into law for it never even reached a vote in the lower house, but in the fact that it marked the beginning of a series of public hearings that the House Committee on Ways and Means conducted with respect to the controversial points of the reduction in rates on Philippine sugar and tobacco. Three separate hearings were held during the year 1905. They were:

[1] For the debate on this bill, H. R. 15702. See *Cong. Record*, 57th Cong., 2nd Sess., pp. 424, 2977, 2981, 2987, 2991, 3001, 3005, 3008, 3066.

First—The Hearings at Washington, D. C. covering the period, January 23 to February 3.

Second—The Hearings in the Philippine Islands before the Secretary of War and the Congressional party, then visiting the islands, during the month of August.

Third—The Hearings again at Washington in the period, December 13-18, 1905.

These public hearings brought out very forcibly and clearly the fundamental objections to the proposals for reduction. Representative Fordney, joint author of the present Fordney-McCumber Tariff Law, fired the opening gun for the opponents of reduction. He told the Committee that his state produced a good deal of sugar from beets and these interests were opposed to the measure. He submitted a letter from the owner of two beet sugar factories in Michigan who characterized the reduction as the "greatest menace" to the beet-sugar industry for the reason that wages in the Philippines amounted to one-tenth of those paid in the United States. In answer to a question from a member of the Committee (Mr. Needham), Mr. Fordney defined his position in the following terms:

So far as doing something for the benefit of the Filipinos is concerned, I am with you all the time, unless it injures an industry in the United States. To reduce the duty on the present amount of sugar coming from the Philippine Islands would be a body blow to the beet sugar and cane sugar industries in the United States, because in the Philippine Islands they can produce sugar to-day, under the present old-fashioned methods, with old-fashioned machinery, without installing farm implements, and paying the present duty and freight rates upon it from the Philippine Islands to San Francisco, and can put it at our markets at 1 cent or more per pound less than it can be produced for in this country.[1]

[1] *Hearings*, Committee on Ways and Means, 58th Cong., 3rd Sess., p. 14.

Still another vocal defender of the sugar interests was found in Mr. W. S. Humphrey, also of Michigan. There had been envisaged in the thoughts of most opponents of the reduction the picture of American capital flowing in a vast stream toward the undeveloped areas of the Philippines and raising enormous quantities of sugar. Prophesies of the future were dragged in as concrete arguments against the proposals for the decrease in duties. Asked if such an outflow of American capital would not be a welcome part of the widely heralded purpose of "benevolent assimilation," Mr. Humphrey replied that it would be and added that what the sugar people could not understand was "how people are [were] so ready to christianize and enlighten all the heathen on the face of the earth at the expense of our home sugar industry." [1]

Representative Fordney and Mr. Humphrey did not constitute the entire sugar contingent. Among the other members of the opposition were the Secretary of the American Beet Sugar Association; the Sebewaing Refining Co., of Sebewaing, Michigan; Mr. David Eccles of Ogden, Utah; Colonel James D. Hill, a sugar planter in New Orleans; and the Secretary of the American Sugar Growers' Association.

Although sugar occupied the center of attention, tobacco and cigars were by no means neglected. The tobacco brigade numbered among its members the President of the New England Tobacco Growers' Association; the President of the National Cigar Leaf Tobacco Association; the President of the Lancaster County Tobacco Growers' Association in Pennsylvania; Representative M. E. Driscoll of the state of New York; and the President of the Cigar Makers' International Union of America, with headquarters

[1] *Hearings*, Committee on Ways and Means, 58th Cong., 3rd Sess., p. 23.

in Chicago, Illinois.[1] A memorandum was submitted by the last organization giving a comparative statement of the labor costs in both countries and ending with a plea against the measure as an act tending to build up the cigar industry of the Philippine Islands at the expense of a like industry in the United States.[2]

Against this array of sugar and tobacco men appeared Colonel Colton, collector of customs of Iloilo, P. I., with a memorial from the Iloilo Chamber of Commerce and Agriculture; Colonel C. R. Edwards, the chief of the Bureau of Insular Affairs in the War Department; and Mr. Taft, the Secretary of War. Answering the fears of the sugar growers and manufacturers, Mr. Taft compared the 83,000 tons sugar production of the Philippines in 1904 with the importation by the United States of 1,847,000 tons in the same year. He took the record year for the sugar production in the Islands when 264,000 tons were produced and declared that such an amount, not all of which could be available for export, would not create a ripple in the price of sugar in the United States. He ridiculed the possibility of a sudden, enormous expansion of the Philippine sugar industry which was pictured by the opponents of the bill, if it became law. "They must calculate," the Secretary of War observed, "the number of acres that under any circumstances could produce sugar and assume that under the proposed change these acres would all be cultivated with the most modern machinery—just as Colonel Sellers calculated the number of people in China that needed eye-water at a dollar a bottle, and he would sell it to them, and he would make four hundred millions of dollars a year."

[1] For these names see *Hearings*, Committee on Ways and Means, 58th Cong., 3rd Sess., *passim*.

[2] *Hearings*, Committee on Ways and Means, 58th Cong., 3rd Sess., p. 104.

Turning to the objections of the tobacco people, he again appealed to the figures. He contrasted the export of 105,000,000 cigars from the Philippines in 1904 with the production of seven billion in the United States. He found this country using 140,000,000 pounds of domestic leaf in making cigars, and the Philippines exporting only 19,000,000 pounds of both filler leaf and smoking tobacco.[1]

A curious twist of Congressional psychology was displayed at one point in the course of the hearings. Representative Franklin S. Brooks, from Colorado, premising his view on the vague and obscure status of the Philippines and America's purpose to work toward an ultimate arrangement other than association with the Union or as an integral part of it, said: ". . . . when we take those islands over we not only have the right, but it seems to me, to some extent at least, we have the duty of protecting our own previously existing enterprises. I do not want to be thought to advocate an unethical system of legislation, but I do not see anything unethical in protecting our own people as compared with those whom we are taking over to beneficently assimilate."[2]

It is a mistake to suppose that those advocating the reduction were doing so in spite of probable injury to America's industries. The father of the bill—H. R. 17752—explicitly stated his belief that it would not result in harm to the people of Michigan or of any state in the Union.[3]

In August of that same year—1905—Secretary of War Taft took a Congressional party to the Philippines to study conditions. As they traveled along the important centers they held public hearings on the tariff question, the naviga-

[1] *Hearings, op. cit.*, pp. 208-209.

[2] *Hearings, op. cit.*, p. 259.

[3] *Hearings, op. cit.*, p. 259.

tion laws, and the general economic conditions in the islands. Native sugar planters appeared with statistics on labor cost and the other items in the cost of production, including interest, freight rates, and insurance charges, all tending to show that even with the reduction Philippine sugar could not go into the American market and compete with American sugar. The Agricultural Association of the provinces of Panay and Negros of the Philippines presented a memorial in favor of the reduction as a measure that would compel the Chinese and Japanese buyers of Philippine sugar to pay higher prices than what they were then willing to pay. It was contended that the prohibitive Dingley rates virtually threw the Philippine producers into the hands of the Chinese and Japanese buyers.[1]

At this juncture the ingenious collector of customs at Manila, Mr. W. Morgan Shuster, offered a scheme designed to get around the obstructions in Congress.[2] He proposed the passage of a statute by the Philippine Commission to refund to the exporters of Philippine products to the United States the duties paid on them. Since these duties were, under the terms of the Act of 1902, turned over to the Philippine treasury there was no danger of incurring heavy financial obligations without the necessary corresponding assets. The tobacco men of the islands sent a deputation to the Governor General strongly endorsing the suggestion in order that the American market might help replace the Spanish market which had been lost through the change in sovereignty. Expressing himself as being heartily in

[1] *Public Hearings on the tariff, etc.*, Manila, Bureau of Public Printing, 1905, pp. 9, 148.

[2] *The Manila American* for February 18, 1905 and *The Manila Times* of February 14, 1905, both quoted in *Exhibit B* of the testimony of D. D. Colcock in *Hearings* before the Committee on Ways and Means, p. 6, 59th Cong., 1st Sess., Gov't Printing Office, Washington, 1906.

favor of opening the home markets to Philippine tobacco the Governor General, nevertheless, pointed out that materialization of the scheme would be apt to cause legislation in Congress hostile to Philippine interests and would put the insular government in the position of opposing Congress.. This effectually put a quietus on the further progress of the plan.

After coming back from its Philippine trip, the Committee on Ways and Means resumed, in the latter part of the same year, —1905,—at Washington the hearings on sugar and tobacco. The war of statistics was reopened with renewed and increased vigor. Mr. Colcock, of the American Cane-Growers Association; Mr. Hathaway, of Saginaw, Michigan; Mr. Hatch, of the Hawaiian Sugar Planters' Association; Mr. Waxelbaum, for the tobacco growing interests of Georgia and Florida; and the Presidents of the United Cigar Manufacturers, with headquarters at New York City, and the Cigar Makers' International Union of Chicago sustained the negative side of the debate: while Mr. Welborn, the chief of the Bureau of Agriculture of the Philippines, with other Government officials, just as strenuously stood for the affirmative. The hearings lasted from December 13 to December 18, 1905. At their conclusion nothing more was known about relative labor costs, the supply of labor in the islands, and the prospects for a greatly increased production than what had already been surmised in the beginning. The elements entering into the question were simple enough. Two of the four important Philippine industries felt the need of decreased duties to help in their slow recovery. Similar industries in the United States objected to the concession because it contained a potential menace in the more or less distant future. Experts were called in. As usual, they disagreed. And both sides waited for the next test of strength in the Capitol.

Previously, on December 29, 1904, the Secretary of the American Beet Sugar Association had sent out a pamphlet entitled "Should the U. S. Tariff on Philippine Sugar and Tobacco be Reduced?"[1] In one of the closing paragraphs that official said:

> . . . Hereafter I will not only thoroughly analyze the attitude and votes of your representatives in both Houses, when they relate to sugar, but I will see that such analyses are placed in the hands of all who have interests at stake, to the end that the thanks received will be of a more specific and widely distributed nature, and, if there should be those who are indifferent to their home interests, those home interests can also show indifference; can see that at the next election they are elected to "stay at home". Surely the votes of 75,000 to 100,000 farmers and as many more laborers, storekeepers, professional men, bankers, etc., who look to this industry either in part or in whole for their income, should be able to keep their friends in Congress.

THE PAYNE BILL, DECEMBER, 1905

On December 4, 1905, Mr. Payne introduced a bill providing, among other things, for reduction of the duties on sugar and tobacco to 25 per cent of the Dingley rates and for free trade in the products of the two countries after the 11th day of April, 1909.[2] When the proposed reduction came up for debate in the House of Representatives the members immediately plunged into the same figures of production costs, wages, freight, and insurance rates, interest, and prices that had been threshed over with such thoroughness and lack of results in the Committee Hearings. The spectacle of the Republican house leaders de-

[1] This pamphlet is inserted in *Hearings* before the Committee on Ways and Means on the Philippine Tariff, 59th Cong., 1st Sess., pp. 273-295.

[2] *H. R. Report*, no. 20, 59th Cong., 1st Sess.

fending a measure looking toward ultimate free trade between the United States and the Philippines provoked sarcastic words of approval from the other side of the chamber and precipitated a lengthy debate on the tariff issue.[1]

Mr. Payne's Philippine bill had the backing of the administration. In his message to Congress, President Roosevelt urged the legislation because of "the agricultural conditions of the Islands." He did not anticipate that free trade would "produce a revolution in the sugar and tobacco production of the Philippine Islands."[2] While the bill was under consideration in the Committee of the Whole, Mr. Fordney, in behalf of the representatives opposing the measure because of its possible menace to the sugar and tobacco industries of the United States, offered the following amendment:[3]

Provided, however, that on all sugars in excess of 200,000 tons, wholly the growth and product of the Philippine Islands, coming into the United States from the Philippine Islands, each calendar year from and after the passage of this act, there shall be levied, collected and paid the full rates of duty as now provided by law on all sugars coming into the United States from foreign countries, other than Cuba and territory belonging to the United States, and that the rate on tobacco shall apply as follows:

	Cigars *Number*	*Wrapper Leaf* *Pounds*	*Filler Leaf* *Pounds*
Free of duty	50,000,000	300,000	3,000,000
At 25% Dingley rates ...	100,000,000	400,000	4,000,000
At 50% Dingley rates ...	150,000,000	No limit	No limit
At 75% Dingley rates ...	200,000,000	No limit	No limit

[1] For the record of the debates, see *Cong. Record*, 59th Cong., 1st Sess., pp. 694, 724, 753, 833 852, 857, 913, 921, 950, 973, 986, 1017, 1085, 1100, 1139.

[2] Quoted in the speech of Mr. Loud, *Cong. Record*, 59th Cong., 1st Sess., p. 1041.,

[3] *Cong. Record*. 59th Cong., 1st Sess., p. 1146.

Commenting on the amendment, the Chairman of the Committee on Ways and Means said:

> . . . I have advocated this bill, not using the terms "square deal" . . . but our "plain duty," that came down to us from President McKinley and give this as a duty we owe to the Philippine people. Now, I do not know what I should think of myself if I should catch myself thinking it was our plain duty to give this concession of tariff up to 300,000 tons and then put up 75 per cent of the Dingley rates on whatever came in beyond that. . . .

At the same time he informed the House that he had consulted nine memebrs of his committee and those nine were opposed to the amendment; that he was authorized by the Secretary of War (W. H. Taft) to say that the Secretary was opposed to the amendment and "would rather have no bill than to have this bill with this amendment." [1]

The amendment was voted down and on January 16, 1906 the bill passed the House of Representatives. Upon reaching the Senate, it was referred to the Committee on the Philippines, in whose files it found a place of oblivion.

THE PAYNE-ALDRICH BILL APPROVED AUG. 5, 1907

This same question of the tariff on Philippine products entering the United States again came up before the Congress as one of the sections of the general tariff bill introduced on March 5, 1909.[2] After seven years of legislative inaction, the result was a measure whose essential features were dictated by the sugar and tobacco interests.[3] While four years previously, Mr. Payne had indignantly rejected the proposition of legislation for free trade within limits,

[1] *Cong. Record*, 59th Cong., 1st Sess., p. 1146.

[2] Sec. 5 of H. R. 1438.

[3] *Supra*, pp. 103-108.

this time he appeared as the reluctant but unabashed sponsor of that section relating to Philippine products which embodied the same principle he had so eloquently inveighed against in 1905. "As far as the limits are concerned," Mr. Payne said, "I would not have put them on, but a majority of the committee favored it." In the next paragraph he further referred to those limits as representing "a sort of a compromise between the friends of the islands and the friends of the sugar beet and other outlying industries. . . ."[1]

A similar complete reversal of opinion with respect to the wisdom of free trade in Philippine products within limits, was witnessed in another friend of the Philippines --W. H. Taft. In 1905 when the same question came up before the House of Representatives he had authorized Mr. Payne to declare on the floor of the House that he (Mr. Taft was then Secretary of War) "would rather have no bill than to have this bill with this amendment."[2] In 1909 the former Secretary of War became the occupant of the White House and had completely changed his view on this same subject.[3]

While the provision relating to Philippine products was being discussed in the House of Representatives the Resident Commissioner for the Philippine Islands stated the position of the Filipino people in the following terms:

If, instead of the free admission without limitation as to quantity of American products into the Philippine Islands, this bill provided only the free entry there of agricultural machinery and other commodities of prime necessity, such as cotton cloth, and which are needed for the agricultural and industrial

[1] *Cong. Record*, 61st Cong., 1st Sess., p. 190.

[2] *Supra*, p. 110.

[3] *Infra*, p. 113.

development of those islands, or if this bill provided only for such reciprocal exchange of commodities custom-duty free as would balance the limited quantity of American products to be sent from here—if such were the provisions of this bill, it would be our pleasant duty as representatives of the Philippine people to make manifest to this House their gratitude. . . . [1]

Representative Fordney, the consistent defender of the sugar industry, this time urged the adoption of the compromise in the following language:

. . . We are trying to do something for the Philippine Islands. Let me tell you what the Philippine Islands are doing for us. I will stand by the bill and the compromise on sugar, the free importation of 300,000 tons per year from the Philippine Islands into the United States.

I am willing to stand by that and the sugar men of the country whom I have consulted are also satisfied. For the last ten years there has been turmoil in this House over the duty on sugar. There never has been a session of Congress in the ten years that I have had the honor to be a Member of this House that the question of the reduction of the duty on sugar has not been advocated in some manner or other, and our present good President has agreed in my presence that during his administration he will not permit as far as he can avoid it by his action, any further reduction in the sugar schedule if we will accept this agreement and let the 300,000 tons come in free from the Philippines. Last year the Philippine Islands exported $60,000,000 worth of stuff and fifteen millions, or 25 per cent, came to the United States. She imported $30,000,000 worth of stuff, and she took the measly sum of $5,000,000 from the United States. It is costing us, if I am correctly informed, $14,000,000 per year to maintain peace in the islands, and if you will look up the record you will find that our pension rolls amount to $23,000,000 annually for Spanish war soldiers. . . . After doing all this for the Philippine

[1] *Cong. Record*, 61st Cong., 1st Sess., p. 931.

Islands, she buys only one-sixth of her imports from us—the measly sum of $5,000,000 of our products—and then comes back and asks us for more, and complains because we reserve the right to tax in excess of 300,000 tons of sugar and tobacco coming in here above the limited amount.[1]

Having the approval of the representatives of the sugar and tobacco interests in Congress, this section of the Payne-Aldrich tariff bill relating to Philippine products found the path of enactment less thorny than before and emerged as a law, with the other sections of the general tariff bill, on August 5, 1909.[2]

It might be well to summarize the contents of this Philippine section of the Payne-Aldrich law. When it finally received Congressional approval, it provided that:

1. All goods, except rice, which are the growth, product, or manufacture of the United States shall be admitted to the Philippines free of duty provided the shipment conforms to certain conditions such as the absence of a drawback of customs duties, etc.

2. All goods, with the similar exception of rice, which are the growth, product or manufacture of the Philippine Islands shall be admitted, free of duty, to the United States under identical canditions plus the added ones that:

(a) the number of cigars admitted in any one year may not exceed 150,000,000; the amount of wrapper tobacco and filler tobacco, when mixed with more than 15 per cent of wrapper tobacco, may not go beyond 300,000 pounds, filler tobacco 1,000,000 pounds, and sugar 300,000 gross tons.

[1] *Cong. Record*, 61st Cong., 1st Sess., p. 333.

[2] For a discussion of the beneficial effects of the law on Philippine foreign trade see D. C. Worcester, *The Philippines Past and Present* (New York, 1913), vol. ii, p. 913 *et seq.*

(b) Not more than 20 per cent of the value of manufactured articles shall consist of foreign materials.

The Payne-Aldrich tariff law[1] thus allowed the free entry of all U. S. products except rice, into the Philippines without limit as to quantity or restriction as to origin. Philippine products, also with the exception of rice, were allowed free entry into the U. S. with the significant exemptions of sugar and tobacco which were to be admitted only up to a certain amount, and Philippine goods which contained more than 20 per cent of foreign material.

THE UNDERWOOD TARIFF ACT OF 1913

By the Underwood Tariff Act of 1913 the limitations on the quantity of sugar and tobacco to be admitted free of duty were removed. Rice from both countries was placed on the free list, a change that was of no significance. The exclusion of Philippine products containing more than 20 per cent of foreign material from the benefits of free entry was retained, apparently because it was not thought of sufficient importance to be changed.[2]

After eleven years of effort the interchange of the articles of trade between America and the Philippines thus came to be unhampered by customs duties except in the case of Philippine products made from foreign raw material. In contemplating the establishment of such trade relations between the two countries, the Chief of the Bureau of Insular Affairs said in 1906:[3]

[1] The debate on section 5 of this law—its Philippine provision—is found in *Cong. Record*, 61st Cong., 1st Sess., pp. 3177-3218, 3227, 3251, 3326-3338, 4185, 4290.

[2] *Report of the Chief of the Bureau of Insular Affairs*, 1913, p. 5.

[3] *Report of the Chief of the Bureau of Insular Affairs*, 1906, pp. 7 *et seq.*

One might think, considering the result of past efforts to obtain this legislation so earnestly desired by the Filipinos, that we were called upon to enter into some altruistic bargain impoverishing our people for the benefit of barbarians on the other side of the earth. It requires very little analysis of the measure to show that it involves no extreme altruism.

There can be no reasonable doubt that if the Philippines were wholly independent of the United States, the trade relations established by this act would be welcomed by our business interests in the United States. Compare the terms of this bill with those of the commercial convention between the United States and Cuba. Which is more favorable to us?

Briefly, in 1902, as a pure business proposition, we admitted to our protected home market with a 20 per cent reduction of the existing tariff 1,000,000 tons of sugar and $14,000,000 worth of tobacco produced in Cuba, for such an opportunity as was given us to sell to Cuba $25,000,000 worth of American goods under a tariff differential varying from 20 to 40 per cent in our favor as against our competitors.

The bill now before the Senate, similarly translated, is an offer to admit to our protected market as much of the sugar and tobacco of the Philippine Islands as may be tempted thereby, but which is naturally limited to the tobacco available for export, an amount that has never exceeded 262,000 tons of sugar (1893) and $2,800,000 worth of tobacco (1902). In exchange for this relatively small concession, an opportunity would be given us to sell in the Philippines $26,000,000 worth of American goods at a 100 per cent differential in our favor over the tariff rates imposed by Congress on the goods of our competitors.

With American consumption of Cuban sugar and tobacco so large in proportion to the maximum production of the Philippines, these figures do not tell the whole story. The tobacco of Cuba has a ready market and is appreciated in the United States. Such is not the case with Philippine tobacco, which is practically unknown in our market and would admittedly find little favor with the American consumer.

In both Cuba and the Philippines this reciprocal arrangement gives us an advantage in supplying such additional demand as will be created by progress and increased prosperity, as well as the present needs of those countries. But the Philippines have five times the population of Cuba, with at present but one-half of the imports which Cuba had in 1902, and it is evident that with fair progress the increase in demand in the Philippine Islands will far exceed that of Cuba.

It should be borne in mind that the increased demand in Cuba means an increase of sugar and tobacco exported to the United States. Such would be the case in the Philippines to but a very slight extent. The increased demand there would depend chiefly on increased exportation of Manila hemp and copra, neither of which competes with any American product, the two forming to-day 75 per cent of the total of Philippine exports, a proportion which is constantly increasing.

A survey of the pending legislation [in 1906] leads inevitably to the conclusion that it is by no means an altruistic measure but one of distinct advantage to us, regardless of its advantage to the Filipinos. It may be safely asserted that in no case have we been able to obtain from any country a reciprocal trade arrangement so favorable to us as that embodied in this bill which increases our home market by over 7,000,000 people, producers exclusively, with the exception of a relatively few cigars and cigarettes, of raw material, and, more important still, of raw material 75 per cent of which competes with no product of the United States, though of great use in our factories.

These considerations refer to the full application of the proposed bill after April 11, 1909. . . .

TARIFF LEGISLATION (1902-1913) ON PHILIPPINE PRODUCTS AS INDICATING ECONOMIC POLICY

The legislation regarding the duties on Philippine products entering the United States furnished a more clean-cut test of America's economic policy toward the islands than the laws that were passed relating to the customs duties on goods imported into the Philippines. While the promotion of American trade had been one of the essential principles in the determination of the customs tariff surrounding the Philippine Archipelago[1] still that phase of economic legislation on the Philippines by the United States Congress never aroused the same thorough and exhaustive discussion that its sister subject—the tariff on Philippine products exported to the United States—actually called forth. This is so because there was agreement as to policy in the one case and a disagreement in the other. And it is precisely because of that divergence of opinion that the purpose behind the resulting legislation becomes fairly clear. American economic interests were united in the desire to capture the Philippine market as against other foreign traders. They were divided when it came to the admission of commodities from the islands in exchange for American goods. That division arose out of the possibility of competition by Philippine sugar and tobacco with the corresponding, protected industries in the United States. It was to no purpose that administration officials continuously pointed out the unlikelihood of any harm resulting from the encouragement of the importation of Philippine products. "During this period," said the Chief of the Bureau of Insular Affairs in 1906[2] everyone connected with the government of the Philippines has been impressed with the urgent need of some such legislation as that proposed, to lift the Filipino people out of the depth of poverty into which they have fallen as the result of the wars, insurrections, and pestilence with which those islands have been cursed for a period of ten years. And not only have they thus agreed to the importance of this legislation to the

[1] *Supra*, ch. iv.

[2] See his report for 1906, pp. 7 *et seq.*

islands, but they have been uniformly of the opinion that such assistance as would be given the depressed agriculture of the Philippines by this act could in no wise harm any interest in the United States."

The revenue act of March 8, 1902 was passed by the House of Representatives in record time and actually went through the Senate with so little delay because of the fear of the importations of Philippine tobacco and sugar after the Supreme Court had pronounced its decision in the Fourteen Diamond Rings case in the latter part of 1901.[1] A nominal reduction of 25 per cent of the Dingley rates was granted—a reduction which Governor Taft and Vice-Governor Wright of the Philippines declared to be entirely inadequate for the purpose of reviving Philippine industry. During the period 1902-1909 American goods coming into the Philippine market were subject to the low tariff schedules erected for the Philippines by the United States Congress and designed to encourage the export and sale of American products, and based on the principle of tariff for revenue.[2] At the same time the Philippine products came into the United States at a 25 per cent reduction from the full rates levied under the Dingley tariff,—a tariff based on the principle of protection.

For seven years, that is to say, from 1902 to 1909, the Administration forces in Congress tried to push through legislation regarding trade relations between America and the Philippines that would more nearly approach that equitable arrangement for reciprocal advantages, which so many professed to have at heart. For the same length of time the sugar and tobacco *bloc* in Congress successfully prevented legislation along those lines. And finally, in the

[1] *Supra*, chs. iii, iv.

[2] *Supra*, ch. iv.

Payne-Aldrich bill of 1909 a compromise was reached and its terms securely safeguarded the tobacco and sugar producers of the United States from the possibility of serious competition from the Islands. It was free trade for American products, except rice, without limit as to quantity; for the Philippine products an exception was made not only as to rice but, also sugar and tobacco, which were to be admitted free of duty only up to a certain amount.[1] Manufactured goods in the Philippines containing over a certain percentage of foreign material were also to be excluded from the free list. Manifestly, the Philippine provision of the Payne-Aldrich bill of 1909 was simply an instance of generosity within limits.

In 1913 the Underwood tariff bill[2] removed the restrictions on the importation of Philippine products except the one regarding manufactured articles with more than 20 per cent of foreign material. No strong opposition appeared against the removal of these limitations.[3] While these provisions of the Underwood tariff law wiped out most of the discriminatory features of section 5 of the Payne-Aldrich law, no less an authority than the head of the Bureau of Insular Affairs had in 1906 said, with respect to a bill containing a provision for free trade:

> It may be safely asserted that in no case have we been able to obtain from any country a reciprocal trade arrangement so favorable to us as that embodied in this bill. . .

If the Philippine section of the Underwood tariff was an act of substantial justice to the Philippines, in the sense that it lessened the injustice of the provisions of the tariff act

[1] *Supra*, p. 113.

[2] Section IV, Par. C.

[3] *Cong. Record*, 63rd Cong., 1st Sess., pp. 1133, 1134.

[4] *Supra*, p. 116.

of 1909, it was also a safe and probably profitable business arrangement for the United States. As much had been admitted as far back as 1906, by the Bureau of Insular Affairs itself.

In an earlier chapter[1] the theory was advanced that the details of Philippine legislation enacted by Congress have been determined on the basis of the realities of American politics. That statement, as obvious as it is general, became illustrated in the concrete in the course of the legislative struggle, which has just been examined, for free trade between America and the Philippines. In this instance, the central reality of the political conflict that was waged was the existence of a *bloc* determined to protect the economic interests of the districts which its members represented.[2]

[1] Chapter iv.

[2] The "Emergency Tariff" of May 27, 1921 as well as the permanent Tariff Act of September 21, 1922 did not change the free trade relations between America and the Philippines except in the sense that Philippine products obtained increased advantages in the American market to the extent of the increase in duties imposed on imports into the United States. See *Public*, no. 10 and *Public*, no. 318, respectively.

CHAPTER VI

The Coastwise Shipping Legislation

The transportation of merchandise and passengers from the Philippines to the United States and *vice versa* furnished another subject for legislation, which raised questions of economic policy. Should the opportunity to handle this carrying trade be restricted to vessels of American registry, or should it be opened to the vessels of all nations? A slightly different form was given to the question by the long-existing statutes on American coastwise trade giving to American vessels a monopoly of that trade. When the subject of Philippine-American commerce was discussed, the question thus became, "Should the United States coastwise shipping laws be extended to the Philippines?" Such extension carried with it the exclusion of foreign ships.

THE TARIFF ACT OF MARCH 8, 1902

Section 3 of the Tariff Act of March 8, 1902,[1] contains the first crystallization of Congressional policy on this subject. The first paragraph provided for the collection of tonnage taxes from foreign vessels engaged in Philippine-American trade and in inter-island commerce in the Philippines. The second postponed until July 1, 1904 the provisions of the U. S. coastwise law "restricting to vessels of the United States the transportation of passengers and merchandise directly or indirectly from one port of the United

[1] *Public*, no. 28, 32 *U. S. Stat. L.*, 54.

States to another port of the United States" in the Philippine-American trade and the inter-island commerce in the Philippines.

In explaining these provisions of the Act, Mr. Payne, Chairman of the Committee on Ways and Means, told his colleagues in the House that the section was made necessary by the decision of the Treasury Department, based on the court decisions on the Insular cases, holding the coastwise laws to be applicable to Porto Rico and the Philippines; and that the lack of American bottoms made the postponement of the operation of those laws with regard to the Philippines imperative. Nevertheless, the Representative from New York hoped that the time would soon come when American citizens would be able to furnish enough American tonnage to carry all the commerce between the Philippines and the United States. When that time had arrived, he and his colleagues on the Republican side would see to it that "these coastwise laws are extended to the ports of the Philippine Islands, as well as to all other ports, that are under the flag of the United States." [1]

In the course of his remarks Senator Lodge, the sponsor for the bill in the Senate and Chairman of the Senate Committee on the Philippines, referred to the tonnage taxes on foreign vessels entering the commerce between America and the Philippines and that between the different islands in the Philippine group. The Senate amendment, he said, to this particular provision of the House bill merely extended those tonnage taxes to cover foreign ships engaged in inter-island trade in the Philippines. That would "necessarily" give, in the words of the Senator, "to any American vessels entering the trade an advantage which they ought to have, for

[1] *Cong. Record*, 57th Cong., 1st Sess., p. 392. See also the speeches of Mr. Grosvenor and Senator Lodge on pp. 354, 825.

it is greatly to our interest to have the inter-island trade pass into American hands at the earliest moment." [1]

It will be remembered that in the House of Representatives the lack of American-owned bottoms had been advanced as one of the arguments for considering the bill as one having the character of an emergency nature, in so far as it concerned shipping in trade between America and the Philippines. In order to separate this issue from others of a more controversial nature, Senator Bacon offered a separate joint resolution [2] providing that the coastwise laws of the United States should not apply to the Philippine Islands until "otherwise provided by law." Nothing came out of his proposed joint resolution and the bill was passed as reported by the Committee on the Philippines.

THE ACT OF APRIL 15, 1904

The Law of March 8, 1902 had postponed the extension of the coastwise laws to the Philippines until July 1, 1904. In April of the latter year another Act was passed superseding the shipping sections of the Act of two years before. The first section of the Act of 1904 restricted the carrying of goods, except in the army and navy, after July 1, 1906, between ports of the United States and of the Philippines, to vessels flying the American flag. The second section had the same inhibition with respect to the passenger transportation. In both sections, severe penalties were inserted in case of violation of their provisons. The third section removed the inter-island trade from the scope of those restrictions.[3]

[1] *Cong. Record*, 57th Cong., 1st Sess., p. 826. Willis, also, mentions this discriminatory provision in his book, *Our Philippine Problem*, p. 286.

[2] S. R. 47, *Cong. Record*, 57th Cong., 1st Sess., p. 1056.

[3] *Public*, no. 114, 33 *U. S. Stat. L.*, 181.

This Law of April 15, 1904 originated as Senate Bill 2259. It was referred to the Senate Committee on the Philippines, the body in the Senate charged with Philippine affairs. In the House of Representatives, however, the bill was given over to the Committee on Merchant Marine and Fisheries, a procedure that was not without significance. The report of the Senate Committee urged the adoption of its amendment to the original bill to exclude inter-island shipping from the operation of the coastwise laws and declared that American tonnage in ample measure existed to serve the needs of Philippine-American commerce.[1] While the Senate Committee submitted a brief and meagre report, that of the House proved to be more copious and informing. On the second page of its report, the various sections of the bill were taken up and a clear exposition made of the intent and purpose of each. When the seventh section was reached giving the Secretary of Commerce and Labor the task of administering the law, the Committee said: "This is a shipping bill primarily. Its purpose is to promote American shipping as well as to regulate Philippine trade. The Secretary of Commerce and Labor should therefore enforce it." And later on the majority of the Committee concluded with these words: "This American service may cost America something; it may cost the Philippines something; but it will be worth while. These American ships will bind the Philippine Archipelago more closely to our country and our government."[2]

Public hearings were held on the bill before the Senate Committee on the Philippines. They afforded an opportunity to ventilate widely varying opinions on the obvious points involved. Were there American ships sufficient in number to carry this trade between the islands and the United

[1] *S. Report* 137, 58th Cong., 2nd Sess.

[2] *H. Report*, 1904, 58th Cong., 2nd Sess., pp. 2, 7, 9.

States? On this point the shipowning and shipbuilding interests replied in the affirmative, while the cordage manufacturers, mostly of the Eastern states, answered with a similarly sweeping and emphatic negative. Would the operation of the law result in increased freightage rates and thus tend to drive the foreign trade of the Philippines to countries other than the United States? During the hearings such probable increase in freight rates was admitted as a certainty even by the representative of the Michigan Steamship Company. Nevertheless, it was thought that with the differentials represented by the tariff and the remission of export taxes on Philippine products exported to the United States, the volume of trade between the two countries would not be affected, inasmuch as the probable increase in shipping rates would not equal the amount represented by the tariff and export tax differential. Much, also, was made of the advantages to the United States of a merchant marine as a naval auxiliary. Beyond the considerations of policy represented by these much-mooted questions, on which there was room for honest differences of opinion, were economic interests which furnished answers that harmonized marvelously well with their specific needs. On one side stood the shipbuilding, shipowning, and allied industries, all of them fully convinced that the measure was one not only in the interest of the American but also of the Filipino people. On the other side were ranged the cordage manufacturers, dealers in agricultural implements, and others under the influence of these two groups. Their representatives opposed the law as one that would not prove to be of benefit, if indeed it did not result in harm, to the United States, and characterized it as unfair to the Filipinos. The heart and the purse strings were in perfect accord.[1]

[1] For these hearings, see *S. Doc.* 124, 58th Cong., 2nd Sess.

In both Houses of Congress this Philippine Shipping Law of April 15, 1904 provoked a more extensive discussion than was had on similar provisions of the Act of March 8, 1902 or the several subsequent acts on the same subject. Senator Carmack, of Tennessee, quoted with approval the report of the Philippine Commission urging the suspension of the operation of the coastwise laws, at least until July 1, 1909, and protesting vigorously against the establishment of the shipping monopoly while such heavy duties, as were being levied, existed on products from the Philippines.[1] Still another Senatorial foe of the measure was Mr. Culberson. He found objection not only to the "indefensible" monopoly that would be created but also to the violation of the open-door policy that was involved in that monopoly. In the preliminary consideration of the treaty with Spain, Senator Culberson observed, "the American commissioners, among them the distinguished author of this bill (Mr. Frye), declared to the Spanish commissioners that the policy of the United States in the Philippines would be that of an open-door to the world's commerce. Necessarily and obviously such a policy would place both the ships and merchandise of all nations upon terms of equality in the Philippines." [2]

This line of argument was further developed in the minority report in the House of Representatives. The report quoted a note of November 23, 1899, by Secretary Hay to the British Ambassador, stating that the policy of the United States in the Philippines would be that contained in annex 2 of protocol 16 of the negotiations at Paris for the treaty of peace. The report went on to explain that this annex was a statement made by the plenipotentiaries of the

[1] *Cong. Record*, 58th Cong., 2nd Sess., p. 2656.

[2] *Cong. Record*, 58th Cong., 2nd Sess., p. 3037.

United States, previous to the signature of the treaty of Paris, as an explanation of that clause of the treaty giving Spanish ships and goods equal rights with those of the United States for a period of ten years. The language of the protocol itself, the minority report quoted as follows:

The declaration that the policy of the United States in the Philippines will be that of an open door to the world's vessels and merchandise on the same footing as American is not intended to be exclusive. But the offer to give Spain that privilege for a term of years is intended to secure it to her for a certain period by special treaty stipulation whatever might be at any time the general policy of the United States.

According to this report of the minority of the House Committee on Merchant Marine and Fisheries, the protocol immediately preceding protocol 16 contained an annex wherein the American peace commissioners offered the provision for equal treatment for Spanish shipping and goods sent to the Philippines with those of the United States, accompanied by a statement that it was "the policy of the United States to maintain in the Philippines an open door to the world's commerce."

Concluding, the minority report said:

It is true that the language of the protocol (protocol 16) expressly recognizes the power of the United States to change its general policy with regard to the Philippines at any time, but a change with regard to the Philippines cannot but be inconsistent so long as the State Department is strenuously insisting upon the general policy of maintaining the open door in the Orient.[1]

Representative de Armond summarized the arguments of

[1] For these arguments see the appendix to *H. Report*, 1904, 58th Cong., 2nd Sess. They are, also, to be found in the speech of Representative Williams in *Cong. Record*, 58th Cong., 2nd Sess., pp. 4440-41.

the opposition when he declared that the effect of the measure would be to create a monopoly for American ship-owners, to increase the price of Philippine articles bought by American consumers, and to lower the prices paid to Philippine producers.[1]

In reply to these arguments, it was held that the bill represented only "an extension of the historic policy" of the American government for nearly a hundred years, which policy was the extension of the navigation laws of the country to its outlying possessions. It was argued that the prices of the Philippine export products would not be affected, since the price of hemp was governed by the world's price and not much sugar or tobacco was imported into the United States. It was urged, furthermore, that passage of the legislation would encourage the flow of American capital and thus be a benefit to the Philippines.[2]

In a short but illuminating passage, Representative Lucking enumerated the interests which were factors in the situation as follows: the cordage manufacturer, the shipping men, the farmer, the exporter, the Filipino, and the broad colonial policy of the government as a whole.[3] The point of view of the shipping interests was typified in an extract from the *Marine Journal* of January 30, 1904, which Senator Lodge inserted as a part of his remarks in the Senate.[4]

The American shipping interest, the *Journal* said, is to be congratulated that there are no treaty obligations with other nations or anything to prevent Congress giving the carrying

[1] *Cong. Record*, 58th Cong., 2nd Sess., p. 4445.

[2] See the speech of Mr. Stevens, *Cong. Record*, 58th Cong., 2nd Sess., p. 4448.

[3] *Cong. Record*, 58th Cong., 2nd Sess., p. 4450.

[4] *Ibid.*, p. 3039.

trade between the Philippines and the United States exclusively to American vessels, and Congress, we believe, can be depended upon to do its full duty to the shipping industry in this particular, as it has done in the past to all other protected industries of the country, notwithstanding the opposition of foreign corporations and their Anglo-American representatives, who had hoped to thrive on the losses that would be sustained by American shipping through lack of proper protective legislation in their interest on the Philippine question.

THE ACT OF APRIL 30, 1906

Two years after the passage of the Act of 1904 providing for the extension of the coastwise laws to the Philippines on the 1st day of July, 1906, another Act was passed further postponing the operation of those laws until April 11, 1909. The bill[1] occasioned little debate and met with practically no serious opposition. The report of the House Committee asserted that there were not enough American ships in the Oriental trade to take care of the commerce of the Philippines and predicted disastrous consequences to Philippine trade in case the coastwise laws were applied.[2] As Chairman of the House Committee on Insular Affairs, Mr. Cooper had charge of the bill. There was very little defense needed and Representative Cooper simply stated it to be the judgment of the Secretary of War, and of every other "disinterested, competent observer" that it was not right to keep a high tariff duty on Philippine exports to the United States and at the same time compel those products to be sent in American bottoms.[3]

That the opinion of business men in the Philippines of all nationalities was in favor of the non-application of the

[1] *H. R.* 18025.

[2] *H. R. Report* 3214, 59 Cong., 1st Sess.

[3] *Cong. Record*, 59th Cong., 1st Sess., p. 5342.

coastwise laws at that time was shown in the report that was submitted at Manila to General Grosvenor, the Chairman of the House Committee on Merchant Marine and Fisheries, on August 19, 1905. The report attacked the Frye Shipping Act (this was the Shipping Act of April 15, 1904) and was signed by the Presidents of the American Chamber of Commerce, the Filipino Chamber of Commerce, the Spanish Chamber of Commerce, and the Chinese Chamber of Commerce; the Acting Secretary of the Manila Chamber of Commerce; the Honorary Secretary of the Shipowners' Association; and three members of the Board of Directors of the Proprietors' Association of Manila.[1]

The bill passed the House by an overwhelming majority and secured the approval of the Senate with practically no debate. It became a law on April 30, 1906.[2]

THE ACT OF APRIL 29, 1908

After the lapse of two years another bill[3] was introduced in Congress to repeal the Act of 1906 and indefinitely to postpone the extension of the coastwise laws to the Philippines. It passed the Senate without debate on March 24, 1908.

Similarly, in the lower chamber, no opposition was voiced on the floor, although a few speeches were made. The chairman of the Committee on Insular Affairs, after remarking that the American shipping companies had had ample notice to meet the requirements of Philippine trade, quoted figures to show that American bottoms carried an almost infinitesimal portion of Philippine-American trade. "So it amounts to a demonstration," the Chairman continued, "that unless we repeal this law there will be a

[1] *Cong. Record*, 59th Cong., 1st Sess., p. 5337.

[2] *Public*, no. 136, 34 *U. S. Stat. L.*, 154.

[3] S. 5626.

marked increase in the freight rates between the Philippines and the United States, and this trade will go elsewhere. There is nothing to compel the Filipinos to trade with this country. There is nothing to compel them to pay the higher freight rates, and it is inevitable, therefore, that the United States would lose much of this trade." [1]

Corroboration of the soundness of this line of reasoning was had from the remarks of Representatives Jones and Williams, both of whom belonged to the Democratic side of the chamber. The latter said he was in favor of the bill because it was much better, both for the Americans and Filipinos, than the law as it then existed, and the former gave it as his opinion that the legislation was demanded "in the interest of the American people as well as that of the Filipinos. . . ." [2]

Such apparent unanimity was reflected in the tremendous majority [3] for this bill to suspend the operation of the coastwise laws in the Philippines indefinitely. It became a statute on April 29, 1908.[4]

When the next shipping legislation came in 1920 there had already transpired profound changes in the economic relations between America and the Philippines. Free trade between the two countries had been established with limitations after 1909 and without those limtations after 1913. A great war had been fought out and that conflict had wrought radical changes in the economic situation of the nations. The United States found itself after the four years of conflict no longer the debtor of the investing nations of Europe but the creditor of the Old World in sums that

[1] *Cong. Record*, 60th Cong., 1st Sess., p. 5080.

[2] *Cong. Record*, 60th Cong., 1st Sess., pp. 5080, 5083.

[3] The vote was: yeas 221 and nays 4.

[4] *Public*, no. 103, 35 *U. S. Stat. L.*, 70.

ran into the billions. A transformation that was quite as complete occurred in her overseas shipping tonnage. Immediately after her entrance into the war, the United States was compelled to engage in a terrific race in which the contestants were the shipbuilding plants of hers (and, indeed, of many nations) and the German submarines, which spread destruction among the shipping fleets of the allies. When the armistice was signed America was the possessor of millions of tons of ocean-going ships actually built, with others still in course of construction in the shipyards. What was to be done with these vessels and in what ways were they to be profitably employed? In time of war and as a vital military measure, the country could afford to lose money in these ships and still regard it as money well spent. But in days of peace the national treasury could not forever make good out of taxes the losses that might be incurred in the operation of a merchant marine. Reduced to the concrete, the question was whether or not American vessels could compete successfully with those of other nations for the world's carrying trade. If the handicap of relatively much higher operating costs was too much for American shipping companies to overcome, what inducements and how much aid could the government offer in order that an adequate merchant marine might be maintained to carry America's products overseas in times of peace and serve as a naval auxiliary in war?

THE MERCHANT MARINE ACT OF JUNE 5, 1920

Congress tried to solve the problem by enacting the Merchant Marine Act of 1920. The portion of the Act that is of concern to us is Section 21 which extends the coastwise laws to all the island territories and possessions of the United States[1] on February 1, 1922. The last proviso,

[1] *Public*, no. 261, 41 *U. S. Statutes*, 997.

however, specified that the extension would not cover the Philippines "until the President of the United States after a full investigation of the local needs and conditions shall, by proclamation, declare that an adequate shipping service has been established . . . and fix a date for the going into effect of the same."

The original bill[1] was a brief document with provisions that did not provoke differences of opinion.[2] In the Senate, however, so many changes were made that the result was a piece of legislation that hardly resembled the original proposition. Among these Senate additions was the one extending the coasting trade provisions of the law to the Philippine Islands and other insular possessions and outlying territories of the United States.[3]

Senator Nelson termed the extension of the coastwise laws "the most wicked and cruel provision of the bill."[4] He opposed this section on the ground that it would have a destructive effect on the commerce of and be a burden to the people of the Philippines, without material effect in securing the products of the Philippines for American trade.[5]

On the other hand, Senator Jones, the one who was chiefly responsible for the legislation on the Senate side, made a strong plea for the adoption of the section extending the costwise laws to the Philippine and other possessions. He would have America take a leaf out of the experience of other nations. He recalled the difficulties met during the world war due to lack of shipping tonnage. He asked the

[1] *H. R. Report* 443, 66th Cong., 1st Sess.

[2] *Cong. Record*, 66th Cong., 1st Sess., pp. 7298, 8052, 8142-8173.

[3] See *S. Report* 573 and the history of *H. R.* 10378 during the second session of the 66th Congress.

[4] *Cong. Record*, 66th Cong., 2nd Sess., p. 6810.

[5] *Cong. Record*, 66th Cong., 2nd Sess., pp. 6810.

question, "How was Great Britain enabled to build up her merchant marine?" And he proceeded to answer his own query by pointing to British colonial legislation in the previous centuries similar in substance to that which he proposed should be enacted by the Congress of the United States. Addressing the chair, the Senator asserted that the trade of the Philippines was for the United States, if she saw fit to take it. He saw no reason why the mother country should not do so, as long as she retained possession of the dependency. "When the opportunity is at hand for us to say that the traffic between those islands and the United States shall be transported in American ships, and thereby build that much trade for American shipping, encourage the building of American ships, and the establishment of American lines across the Pacific, where we need them so badly, why," he asked, "should we not do it?"

He gave it as his opinion that the United States should take the Philippine trade when she could and hold it. It did not mean, in his thoughts, injury to the Philippine Islands. For were there not specific provisions postponing the operation of the section for one year, directing the Shipping Board to provide adequate shipping facilities with proper rates, and finally, giving the President discretionary power to enforce or postpone the operation of this provision?

Waxing enthusiastic, the Senator drew on his imagination and saw ships,—"passenger ships, combination passenger and cargo ships, ships suitable for any ocean-carrying trade"—laden with American products, plying between America's continental ports and Manila, which would become the "great distributing point" for American goods destined to the Far East. "From every standpoint of American interest, the interests of the Philippines, and for the building up of our American merchant marine, it seems to me," he concluded, "that it is wise, judicious and patriotic to extend the coastwise laws to the Philippine Islands." [1]

Senator Simmons thought the bill, by making American competition with foreign ships in the Philippines' foreign commerce possible, would benefit both the Philippines and the United States.[2] Senator Thomas deplored the monopoly in both passenger and freight transportation that would be created, mentioned the probability of retaliation by foreign nations, and argued that if independence was to be given to the Philippines in a few years, she should not, in the interval, be considered as a domestic territory of the United States.[3]

The Senator from New York (Senator Calder) thought the section[4] was a "splendid thing for the merchant marine," and for that reason was very strongly in its favor. In his closing remarks, just before the Senate voted on this section, Senator Jones quoted one of the two resident commissioners from the Philippines as having said in answer to the question, "If we should furnish you ample and adequate American shipping, would you be satisfied to have out coastwise laws applied?" that he, personally, would be satisfied and thought "it would be a good thing." [5]

After extended conferences between the two Houses of Congress, the bill finally emerged as a law and the provision for the extension of the coastwise laws to the Philippines and other island territories and possessions of the United States came out as Section 21 of this Merchant Marine Act

[1] For the remarks of Senator Jones, see *Cong. Record*, 66th Cong., 2nd Sess., pp. 6811, 6812.

[2] *Ibid.*, pp. 6812, 6814.

[3] *Cong. Record*, 66th Cong., 2nd Sess., pp. 6860-6862.

[4] Section 23 in the Senate bill.

[5] After the passage of the law and due to the widespread opposition in the Islands, the Resident Commissioner changed his attitude.

of June 5, 1920. The section provided for extension to the Philippine Islands after a proclamation by the President, declaring that an adequate shipping service has been established and fixing a date for the carrying out of this provision of the law. At the time of writing (February, 1923) and, probably, because of the strenuous opposition of the natives of the Philippines, the President has not yet issued the proclamation.

CHAPTER VII

Public Lands, Franchises, and the Public Debt

THE PROBLEM STATED

In its report dated November 30, 1900, the Taft Philippine Commission estimated the total land area of the Philippine Islands to be approximately 29,694,500 hectares, or 73,345,415 acres. Of this amount 2,000,000 hectares, or about 4,944,000 acres were thought to be owned by individuals, leaving in public lands 27,694,500 hectares or 68,405,415 acres.[1] These lands, which constituted the public domain, formerly belonged to the crown of Spain and title to them had been transferred to the United States Government with the ratification of the Treaty of Paris. Here was a subject for legislation of transcendent importance. During the two years in which the President had full control over the islands by virtue of his war power as Commander in Chief, it was the consensus of opinion that great as his authority was, it did not go beyond the use of the necessary and proper means to carry out the aim of the military operations, which was the pacification of the islands. The question, therefore, of the disposal of the immense amount of public lands and the granting of permanent rights therein could not be said to be within the scope of the President's military power, inasmuch as that power would of itself be extinguished with the disappear-

[1] *Rept. of Taft Phil. Commission* for Nov. 30, 1900 (Gov't Printing Office, Washington, 1901), p. 33.

ance of the conditions that called for its exercise. In the words of Senator Daniel of Virginia:

> . . . whatever was necessary to be done under the principle that the public safety was the supreme law may be done by the conquering general; but the power to do it ceases with the necessity, and any franchise or any privilege or any extraordinary power exercised under the necessity of military law would die of itself with the conditions which created it.[1]

THE FIRST SPOONER BILL

On January 11, 1900, Senator Spooner introduced a bill designed to vest in the President authority to govern the Philippines after the suppression of the insurrection and until Congress otherwise provided. This project of law provided

> that when all insurrection against the sovereignty and authority of the United States in the Philippine Islands . . . shall have been completely suppressed by the military and naval forces of the United States, all military, civil, and judicial powers necessary to govern the said islands shall, until otherwise provided by Congress, be vested in such person or persons and shall be exercised in such manner as the President of the United States shall direct for maintaining and protecting the inhabitants of said islands in the free enjoyment of their liberty, property, and religion.[2]

What was the purpose in the introduction of such a measure in the Senate of the United States? Senator Lodge, the Chairman of the Committee on the Philippines, thought the bill to be an "assertion of Congressional authority and of the legislative power of the Government." He believed

[1] *Cong. Record*, 56th Cong., 2nd Sess., p. 2960. See also *Rept. of the Taft Phil. Commission*, p. 34.

[2] *Cong. Record*, 56th Cong., 1st Sess., p. 763.

the enactment of further legislation would be a great mistake but deemed it important that the Congressional position should be defined and thoroughly understood by the inhabitants of the Philippines, as well as of the United States.[1] The author of the measure, Senator Spooner, declared it to be his purpose to show, by the bill, that Congress was behind the Administration and "put this measure of authority behind the President. . . ." "To leave it [the government of the Philippines] all to his war power,," Senator Spooner said, "semed to him unjust."[2] As is the case with so many other bills, this one failed to reach a vote at that session of Congress and the Spooner bill was reborn later with a different make-up in the legislation known as the Spooner Amendment to the Army Appropriation Act of March 2, 1901.[3]

THE SPOONER AMENDMENT

But, although the second measure was introduced by the same author and, in its first paragraph, repeated almost entirely the Spooner bill of the previous year, the additional provisions, as well as the debates thereon, and certain governmental reports, indicated that the main purpose was no longer to "assert the authority of Congress" and back up the Administration. Rather the aim seemed to be to grant to the President of the United States or his agents the power to make laws and establish rules and regulations of a more or less permanent nature, bearing on several phases of the economic life of the Philippines, in order that pacification might be advanced and economic progress started.

[1] *Cong. Record,* 56th Cong., 1st Sess., p. 2617.

[2] *Cong. Record,* 56th Cong., 1st Sess., p. 2617.

[3] 31 *U. S. Stat. L.,* 910.

The original text of the Spooner Amendment differed from the Spooner bill of the previous year in two points. The power sought to be granted was to be given to the President immediately after passage of the law and not, as in the former bill, after the suppression of the insurrection; and there was an addition of the reservation of the right to "alter, amend, or repeal" all franchises granted under the authority of the Spooner Amendment.

Just what gave rise to this move for immediate authorization to the President to exercise all powers of civil government with the slight limitation as to franchises, as disclosed in the first text of this Amendment, and to the still more drastic course of tacking it on to an army appropriation bill is, though certainty be lacking, perhaps, sufficiently obvious. The very mention of the term "franchises" with the accompanying limitation must be regarded as a specific intent to grant all power legitimately exercisable within the limitation. That the *motif* of the legislation was this very desire to hasten the economic development of the islands is still more convincingly shown in the reports and messages of the Philippine Commission and the Secretary of War in the period from November 30, 1900 to January 24, 1901. The Spooner Amendment was introduced on February 8, 1901.[1] In its report for November 30, 1900 the Taft Philippine Commission said:

> . . . The Commission has received a sufficient number of applications for the purchase of public lands to know that large amounts of American capital are only awaiting the opportunity to invest in the rich agricultural field which may here be developed. In view of the decision that the military government has no power to part with the public land belonging to the United States, and that that power rests alone in Congress,

[1] *Cong. Record*, 56th Cong., 2nd Sess., p. 2117.

it becomes very essential, to assist the development of these islands and their prosperity, that Congressional authority be vested in the government of the islands to adopt a proper public-land system, and to sell the land upon proper terms. There should, of course, be restrictions preventing the acquisition of too large quantities by any individual or corporation but those restrictions should only be imposed after giving due weight to the circumstances that capital cannot be secured for the development of the islands unless the investment may be sufficiently great to justify the expenditure of large amounts for expensive machinery and equipment.[1]

In transmitting this report of the Philippine Commission to the President, the Secretary of War wrote on January 24, 1901:

On the 2nd day of January the Commission as a body re-enforced the views contained in this report by the following dispatch from Manila:

"*Root, Secretary of War, Washington:*

"If you approve, ask transmission to proper Senators and Representatives of following: Passage of Spooner bill at present session greatly needed to secure best result from improving conditions. Until its passage no purely central civil government can be established, no public franchises of any kind granted, and no substantial investment of private capital in internal improvements possible. All are needed as most important step in complete pacification. . . . Power to make change should be put in hands of President to act promptly when time arrives to give Filipino people an object lesson in advantages of peace. . . .

"Sale of public lands and allowance of mining claims impossible until Spooner bill. Hundreds of American miners on ground awaiting law to perfect claims. More coming. Good element in pacification. Urgently recommend amend-

[1] *Report of Taft Philippine Commission*, Nov. 30, 1900, p. 34.

ment Spooner bill so that its operation be not postponed until complete suppression of all insurrection, but only until in President's judgment civil government may be safely established." [1]

Summarizing the points in this recommendation by the Philippine Commission the Secretary of War said. "The army has brought the Philippines to the point where they offer a ready and attractive field for investment and enterprise, but to make this possible there must be mining laws, homestead and lands laws, general transportation laws, and banking and currency laws." [2]

That these recommendations by those charged with the task of administering the affairs of the Philippines had much to do with the introduction and passage of the Spooner Amendment was not only an inference well within reason but also a conclusion specifically stated in the remarks of Senators Hoar, Tillman, Bacon and Turner.[3] The last named Senator asserted as the sole reason for the offering of the amendment that there was no power in the Philippines to dispose of the lands and mines as well as to grant franchises which could be permanent; for "those are the only objects to be accomplished by the passage of this amendment which cannot be accomplished now by the President of the United States as Commander in Chief of our armies." [4]

Defense of the measure consisted in arguments showing the need of taking the judgment of men who were on the spot and who, therefore, presumably possessed much better information than the members of Congress and the proba-

[1] *Report of Taft Philippine Commission*, Nov. 30, 1900, pp. 5-6.

[2] *Ibid.*, p. 7.

[3] *Cong. Record*, 56th Cong., 2nd Sess., pp. 2956-2980, 3067, 3120.

[4] *Cong. Record*, 56th Cong., 2nd Sess., p. 3067.

bility of the measure aiding in the development of the islands, as well as in their pacification.[1]

Objection to the grant of unlimited authority to the President was met with the attempt to establish a parallel with the legislation for the Louisiana territory conferring sweeping powers on the Executive even during the time of that Democrat *par excellence,* Thomas Jefferson. On the other hand, opponents of the Spooner Amendment refused to see any parallelism between the two cases. They stoutly assailed it for its almost unlimited grant of power, its transgression of the doctrine of the separation of powers, and its opening of the door to exploitation and carpet bag rule. Unpleasant reminiscences of the reconstruction period after the Civil War led Southern Congressmen to denounce the Amendment as a vicious attempt at exploitation.[2]

The affirmative side winced under these vigorous assaults. Radical modifications resulted. Indeed, the changes were so great that the final result bore simply an outward resemblance to the original proposition. Originally, the President was to have been given "all military, civil, and judicial powers necessary to govern the Philippine Islands" with the sole limitation that all franchises granted should contain "a reservation of the right to alter, amend, or repeal"; but in the law as finally passed there were the additional stipulations with regard to franchises that they could be granted only with the express approval of the President and when, in his judgment, the grant was "clearly necessary for the immediate government of the islands and indispensable for the interest of the people thereof" and could not "without great public mischief, be postponed until the establishment of permanent civil government." More-

[1] *Cong. Record,* 56th Cong., 2nd Sess., pp. 2963, 3331-3384.

[2] *Cong. Record,* 56th Cong., 2nd Sess., pp. 2957-2963, 2964, 2976.

over, all franchises must terminate one year after the creation of permanent civil government. Severe as were these restrictions on franchise grants, those affecting public lands, timber, and mines were even more so. For there was the categorical prohibition against the " sale, lease, or other disposition " of the public lands, timber and mines.[1]

Thus, what was originally conceived as a measure that would blossom out as Congressional authorization for the disposal of public lands, timber, and mining rights, and the right to grant franchises, eventually turned out to be an explicit prohibition with respect to the first proposition and restrictions amounting almost to a prohibition with regard to the second. The mountain had labored and brought forth something much smaller than a mouse.

THE ORGANIC ACT OF JULY 1, 1902

Congressional legislation with respect to public lands, timber, mining rights, and franchises finally came into being as a part of the bill entitled, " A bill temporarily to provide for the administration of the affairs of the civil government in the Philippine Islands, and for other purposes ", passed on July 1, 1902,[2] and designed primarily for the establishment of civil government in the Philippines. While on its face, as shown by its title and also by the declarations of the chief author himself—Senator Lodge[3]— the bill semed to be meant in the main to establish civil government, the question of the public lands and franchises could not have been very far back in the background. The Philippine Commission in its report for 1901 had renewed its request for power, with restrictions, to grant franchises and to

[1] For the text of the Spooner Amendment, see 31 *U. S. Statutes* 910.

[2] S. bill 2295, 57th Cong., 1st Sess. The law is found in 32 *U. S. Stat. L.*, 691.

[3] *Cong. Record*, 57th Cong., 1st Sess., p. 5031.

enact a public land law. "In the development of these islands it is essential that opportunity shall be afforded for the sale and settlement of the enormous tracts of public lands," [1] the Commission said. And the Senate Committee on the Philippines, in favorably reporting the bill declared that there was "immediate necessity for some legislation in regard to the public lands, and especially in regard to the forests in the islands. . . ." [2] Farther on, the same report asserted that the presence of many mining prospectors in the Philippines made mineral-land legislation necessary. And the report of the House Committee on Insular Affairs affirmed that one of the greatest needs of the islands was the development of their vast natural resources. "For this purpose," the Committee said, "capital must be induced to go to the Philippines, but only under such circumstances and so controlled and regulated by law as to prevent their undue exploitation." [3]

Turning to the debate on the public land,[4] mining, and franchise provisions of the bill we find Senator Lodge as its official sponsor and defender. He said the mining provisions had been prepared with great care by the Philippine Commission, and revised by a subcommittee of the Senate Committee on the Philippines. From his point of view as a layman, the Senator thought those mining provisions were as good as those of any existing statute on the subject. Passing to the subject of public lands, he stated that his committee deemed it a necessity that a proper public land law should be enacted. The Philippine Commission, Mr.

[1] *Report of Phil. Commission* for 1901, pp. 29-30.

[2] *S. Report* 915, 57th Cong., 1st Sess.

[3] *H. Report* 2496, 57th Cong., 1st Sess.

[4] Professor Willis has an interesting discussion of the connection between the sugar trust and public land legislation in his book, *Our Philippine Problem*, pp. 367-368.

Lodge added, was to be given authority to consider and approve regulations for carrying out the provisions of the Act. Provision had also been made for granting titles to squatters. The sections dealing with timber lands were equally well guarded. Concluding, the Senator said:

The main object of the bill . . . is, in a word, to replace military by civil government. . . .

The second object of the bill is to help the development of the islands, and yet, as the committee felt, to help that development only by taking the utmost pains that there should be no opportunity given for undue or selfish exploitation.[1]

Continuing the argument for the affirmative, Senator Stewart thought the bill provided an opportunity for giving an "object lesson" in "enterprise and business." To the Senatorial mind enterprise and business were the main props of civilization. The bill would make it possible for Americans to acquire lands and mines, to engage in business and make contracts in the Philippines, thus supplying that enterprise which would introduce civilization into the Philippines.[2]

Practically no objections were urged against the mining provisions of the bill, in themselves. Criticism centered around these points:

First—That the Filipino people had not been given participation in the decision as to these highly important matters. This point was made by Senators Bacon, Wellington and Clay.

Second—That the quantity of land proposed in the Senate bill for homesteads and for sale or lease to corporations was excessively large. This objection was so widespread

[1] *Cong. Record*, 57th Cong., 1st Sess., pp. 5030-5031.

[2] *Cong. Record*, 57th Cong., 1st Sess., p. 5350.

that it even found converts in Senators Lodge and Stewart, who had defended the original bill.[1]

Third—That the bill furnished an opportunity for the exploitation of the islands. This charge appeared unequivocally in Senator Patterson's speech [2] and was reiterated in a more vehement and dramatic fashion in that of Senator Pettus. Harking back to post-civil war days in the South, Mr. Pettus, figuratively pointing an admonitory finger at his colleagues, said:

> Most of the Senators never lived under a carpetbag government; but those of you who have been governed by carpetbaggers cannot fail to see what will be the effect of this bill when enacted.
>
> If this bill be enacted, and you could and did give to the real carpetbagger his choice to go to heaven or the Philippine Islands, he would not hesitate. He would say promptly, "I will go to the Philippines." [3]

Substantially the same arguments came up in the House when the bill reached that body.[4] The final provisions with regard to public lands in this Act of July 1, 1902 may be summarized as follows:

Section 12 transferred to the Philippine government all property and other rights in the Philippines acquired by the United States from the Kingdom of Spain through the Treaty of Paris.

Section 13 empowered the Philippine government to classify, acocrding to agricultural character and productiveness, and to make rules and regulations regarding the disposal of, the public agricultural lands in the Philippines. Such

[1] *Cong. Record*, 57th Cong., 1st Sess., p. 5354.

[2] *Ibid.*, p. 5967.

[3] *Ibid.*, p. 6145.

[4] *Ibid.*, pp. 7411-7414, 7447-7464.

rules and regulations required approval by the President and submission to Congress and were to become effective upon the failure of Congress to amend or disapprove.

Section 14 made provision for the issuance of free patents to actual holders of land, who did not possess title to them.

Section 15 authorized the granting or sale of public, agricultural lands by the Philippine government in amounts of not more than 16 hectares (40 acres) to a person or 1024 hectares (2560 acres) to a corporation. Sales were to be canditioned on occupancy, improvement, or cultivation of the lot.

Section 16 gave the preference in the grant or sale of public lands to actual occupants and settlers. No public lands in actual possession of a native could be sold without his consent. The prior right given to an occupant of the land, however, when possession was the only proof of title, was not to extend to more than 16 hectares (40 acres) in one tract.

Section 17-18 dealt with the protection of forests, the enactment of forest laws, and the issuance of timber licenses.

Section 19 defined the basis of water priviliges and empowered the Philippine government to make rules and regulations for the use of water and the protection of the water supply.

Section 20-62 conditioned the provisions relating to mining and mining rights.

Section 75 prohibited corporations from engaging in the real estate business or owning more land than was reasonably necessary to carry out their purposes. Agricultural corporations were limited to the ownership and control of land not exceeding 1024 hectares (2560 acres), and no corporation, except those organized for irrigation, and no member of a mining or agricultural corporation, could be interested in any other corporation engaged in agriculture or mining. Corporations loaning funds on real estate security could purchase real estate when necessary for the collection of loans but such real estate were to be disposed of within five years.[1]

THE ACT OF FEB. 6, 1905

The Act of Congress of February 6, 1905 made practically no serious changes in the land and mining laws in force in the Philippines.[2]

THE ACT OF AUGUST 29, 1916

The Philippine Autonomy Act of 1916 furnished the last occasion for a Congressional pronouncement relative to public lands in the Philippines. Section 9 of that Act gave the Philippine Legislature power to enact legislation for lands of the public domain, and timber and mining lands, subject to a qualified veto by the Governor-General, as is the case with all other legislation, but with the added restriction of approval by the President of the United States, within six months of the enactment and submission of the proposed law.[3]

THE FRIAR LANDS

A main cause of civil disturbance during the Spanish régime in the Philippines had been the agrarian problem presented by large tracts of land owned by the religious orders in the islands. These lands amounted to 400,000 acres in round numbers and were among the most valuable and productive in the country. They were leased to thous-

[1] For these provisions, see the Act of July 1, 1902, 32 *U. S. Stat. L.*, 691.

[2] 33 *U. S. Statutes* 689.

[3] Sec. 9 of *Public*, no. 240, 39 *U. S. Statutes* 545.

ands of tenants and friction between these tenants and the friar landowners was intense. In the period covered by the revolution against Spain and the later developments of the Spanish-American war, the friars were driven from their estates and the tenants totally disregarded the rights of ownership of the religious corporations.

When the American government became responsible for the maintenance of order and the protection of individual rights, including those of property, the friar lands question became one of the most difficult of settlement. The government could not arbitrarily disregard the claims of title, and the rights that go with the ownership of property, by these religious orders. On the other hand, to reestablish the friars in their estates, would, it was believed, seriously endanger the peace and order of the regions affected and earn for the government the hatred of the thousands of tenants involved.

In referring to these friar lands, the report of the Philippine Commission for the year ending October 15, 1901, said:

"The Commission renews its recommendations of last year that it be given authority to issue bonds with which to buy up the agricultural holdings and other property of the religious orders. Now that peace is being restored and civil courts are exercising ordinary jurisdiction, the necessity for removing this firebrand from the important provinces of Cavite, Laguna, Rizal, Bulacan, and Bataan cannot be overstated." [1]

THE FRIAR LANDS NEGOTIATIONS

In furtherance of such a purpose, the Secretary of War sent Civil-Governor Taft, who was then on a visit to the

[1] *Report of the Philippine Commission* for year ending October 15, 1901, p. 24.

United States, a letter of instructions dated May 9, 1902.[1] By it the Civil-Governor was authorized to visit Rome on his way to the Philippines and ascertain what church authorities were empowered to negotiate for and decide upon a sale of the lands. Should Governor Taft find the church officials at Rome possessed of such power, he was to endeavor to attain the results desired, with a reservation for subsequent approval of the agreement by the United States Congress. In conducting the negotiations, the Civil-Governor would regard the following propositions as fundamental:

1. That under the American government the State is separate from the Church.

2. That there existed in the Philippine Islands a novel situation and one which called for adjustment.

3. That the Church could no longer act for the State in public instruction and charities, and conditions called for the abolition of the landed proprietorship of the religious orders in the Philippines in the interests of the Church as well as of the State.

4. That it was the wish of the government, subject to authorization by Congress, to extinguish the titles of religious order to these large tracts with provisions for full and fair compensation.

5. That it was not deemed to the interest of the Filipinos to have such sums paid as compensation used to enable the religious orders to return the friars to the rural parishes.

6. That the titles to church lands and buildings which were in dispute were to be settled fairly.

7. That provision would be made for rentals of church buildings which had been or were occupied by the United States Army.

[1] *See Appendix O, Report of Secretary of War*, 1902, vol. i, pp. 233-261.

8. That rights and obligations under specific trusts for education and charity which were in controversy would be settled by agreement, if possible.

The instructions cautioned Governor Taft that his mission was not "in any sense or degree diplomatic in its nature" but a purely business one conducted by him as Governor of the Philippines for the purpose of acquiring property from their owners. This was quite understandable when taken in connection with the theory that the Church and State move in entirely separate orbits.

The Civil-Governor, also, bore a letter of credentials from the American Department of State addressed to the Papal Secretary of State in which Mr. Taft was presented as Civil-Governor of the Philippines.[1] On June 5, 1902 Governor Taft was received in private audience by the Pope. He presented an autograph note of personal greeting from President Roosevelt and, also, eight bound volumes of the President's literary works.[2]

In stating the object of his visit, Governor Taft said:

> On behalf of the Philippine government it is proposed to buy the lands of the religious orders with the hope that the funds thus furnished may lead to their withdrawal from the islands, and, if necessary, a substitution therefor, as parish priests, of other priests whose presence would not be dangerous to public order. It is further hoped that church titles, rentals, and prices might all be fixed either by arbitration or in a general compromise.[3]

Replying to the proposal of Governor Taft, the Papal Secretary of State recognized the conciliatory effect among the Filipinos of a sale of the estates and announced the

[1] *Report, Secretary of War, op. cit.*, p. 236.

[2] *Ibid.*, p. 236.

[3] *Ibid.*, p. 238.

adherence in principle by the Holy See to the request made by the American government with a reservation as to the rights of property of legitimate possessors and a just and equitable valuation. In view of the complicated nature of the question, the note went on, the Holy See was prepared to give the necessary instructions to the new apostolic delegate to be sent to the islands in order that a satisfactory accord might be arrived at both as to the value of the land and the conditions of the sale.[1]

On July 3, 1902 Mr. Taft submitted his counter-reply with the draft of a proposed agreement. The draft provided for:

1. The purchase by the Philippine government of "all the agricultural lands, buildings, irrigation plants and other improvements" of the Dominican, Augustinian, and Recoleto orders, the price to be fixed by a tribunal of arbitration composed of five members. Two of the members were to represent the Pope, two the Philippine government, and the fifth was to be chosen by a neutral.

2. The delivery by the Philippine government of church lands or enclosures upon which Roman Catholic churches and convents stood and which had not been deeded or formally conveyed by Spain to the Church, without prejudice, however, to the claims of title by the municipality to such land, to be determined in the ordinary courts of law.

3. The reaching of an accord between the Philippine Government and the Holy See with respect to charitable, educational, and other trusts. Failure to reach an agreement would mean submission of the issue to the tribunal of arbitration.

4. The payment of reasonable rentals for church buildings occupied by United States troops. Information for

[1] *Report, Secretary of War, op. cit.*, p. 242.

the use of both parties was to be ascertained by the tribunal provided for in the other sections. The Secretary of War would undertake to present to Congress a request for authority and means to pay such rentals.

These terms were to be accompanied by the following stipulations:

1. That the titles of the religious orders to the lands should be conveyed by deeds in the usual and proper form to the Philippine government before the purchase price was paid.

2. That all the members of the four religious orders were to withdraw from the islands within a certain period of time. In the meantime and before the withdrawal, no member of the orders should go out to do any parish work in the parishes of the Archipelago, except those who had continually discharged parish duties outside of Manila since August, 1898. During two years, a sufficient number could remain to conduct schools, the university, and conventual churches. No Spanish member of the orders was thereafter to be sent to the islands.

3. That except as provided in the above paragraph and in the Jesuit missionary parishes, only secular priest or non-Spanish members of the religious orders whose presence would not disturb the peace or order of the parish were to be appointed as parish priests.[1]

In his rejoinder, Cardinal Rampolla, the Papal Secretary of State, had no objection to the economic provisions, but demurred to the proviso regarding the withdrawal of the religious orders. In the letter, the Holy See stated her policy to be to try to induce members of religious orders of other than Spanish nationality, especially those of the United States, to go to the Philippines. The Holy See

[1] *Report, Secretary of War, op. cit.*, pp. 250-252.

agreed, further, to enjoin all the members of religious orders from taking part in political questions or opposing the established order. These undertakings were embodied in a "Counter Project of Convention," proposed by the Cardinal and which was referred by Governor Taft to the Secretary of War at Washington.[1]

The cabled reply of the Secretary was as follows:

> The reasons making withdrawal desirable are not religious or racial, but arise from political and social relations which existed under the former government, and which have created personal antipathies menacing to the peace and order of the community.
>
> It is the desire to accomplish the removal of this cause of disturbance and discord that had led me to approve that clause of your proposal which would involve the government of the Philippines in a large and undefined obligation, for the purchase of lands in advance of a specific ascertainment of their values, and of the estimated prices which we can reasonably expect to receive from them when we in turn offer them for sale; and to the clauses which would anticipate the authority of Congress in regard to the ascertainment of rentals and damages in the course of occupation, and the conveyance of church lands provided for in your proposal. If this object is not assured, then the arrangement sought should be quite different in form, and should more closely follow the suggestions of Cardinal Rampolla in his memorandum of June 22. . . .[2]

The memorandum referred to was the one in which the Cardinal suggested the conducting of the negotiations at

[1] *Report, Secretary of War, op. cit.*, pp. 252-256.

[2] *Ibid.*, pp. 256-259. In the final settlement it was tacitly understood that the policy of the Papacy would be to withdraw the Friars of Spanish nationality. See Elliot, *The Philippines to the End of the Commission Government* (Indianapolis, 1916), p. 49.

Manila with the apostolic delegate who would be given the necessary instructions by the Church. This plan was followed and Monsignor Jean Baptiste Guidi, archbishop of Stampoli, who received the appointment as apostolic delegate, reached Manila in the autumn of 1902 and there ensued an active resumption of negotiations. In 1901 the Philippine government had asked a surveyor of standing and experience to survey the friar lands and classify and assess them. By 1902, this had been done for all the estates, except two relatively small parcels, the values of which were determined by the Philippine Commission from other sources. From February 16 to March 20, 1903 there were hearings on the valuation of the estates.

Upon further investigation, it developed that the Dominican order had conveyed the title to their lands to an Englishman in Manila, under a promoter's contract, and the latter had organized the "Philippine Sugar Estates Developing Co." for the purpose of taking charge of the property; that the Augustinians had made a similar arrangement with a Spanish corporation named "Sociedad Agricola de Ultramar;" and that the Recoletos had also conveyed the "Imus" estate to the "British Manila Estates Co.," a corporation organized under the laws of either Hongkong or Great Britain. The title to and possession of the Mindoro estate, however, remained with the Recoleto order. These things added complications to the problem facing Governor Taft and his colleagues on the Philippine Commission.

Mr. Taft found it difficult to discover exactly the relation which the orders held to the property which they had ostensibly transferred to corporate hands. That they retained a substantial interest was evident but its nature was most ambiguous. Finally, Governor Taft sent a letter to the apostolic delegate containing a request for a statement of the interst retained by the religious orders in the friar lands. In relating this incident of the negotiations, Governor Taft said: " No formal answer to this letter was ever received, but informally it was stated to me by the delegate that the authorities in the Philippines had informed him that they had so disposed of their interests that they were unable to make a statement of what their interests were, if any." [1]

Then, in a letter of July 5, 1903, Governor Taft offered, with the approval of the Commission, to pay the sum of $6,043,219.07 which represented the valuation that had been set by the surveyor-expert engaged by the Philippine government. Mr. Taft took occasion to state that the motive actuating the government was political and not pecuniary. The members of the Commission, he said, were convinced the transaction would involve a financial loss to the government. " What the government proposes," he stated, " is to buy a lawsuit, and something more than a lawsuit, an agrarian dispute." [2]

This offer of Mr. Taft was rejected and the apostolic delegate suggested ten and a half million dollars as a price that might be acceptable. Governor Taft declined to entertain the suggestion. A few months later, Mr. McGregor, of the " British Manila Estates Co.," said he thought eight and a half milion dollars might prove satisfactory to both sides. After rejecting this proposal, Mr. Taft made a final offer of an increase of one and a half million dollars beyond his first figure and this was ultimately accepted. Due to the fact that two small parcels were found to be already under contract of sale, when the parties reached an agreement on December 3, 1903, the contract provided for the

[1] *Report of the Philippine Commission* (1903), pt. i, p. 40.

[2] *Ibid.*, p. 42.

purchase for $7,239,784.66, with a provision that the sum to be paid would be proportionately reduced in case the surveys showed that the lands were smaller than the area mentioned in the contract. So that when the Philippine government made the last payment on October 20, 1905, the total payments amounted to $6,934,433.36.[1]

It has already been noted that Governor Taft had expressly affirmed in his first offer that the object of the government was political rather than pecuniary; that the motive behind the purchase was the hope of settling a serious agrarian dispute. If this was true of the intentions of the Philippine government officials it was not less so in the case of the legislators at Washington who were charged with the task of preparing the legislation in order that the transaction could be consummated. This piece of legislation emerged as Sections 63, 64, and 65 of the Act of July 1, 1902 entitled "An Act Temporarily to provide for the administration of the affairs of civil government in the Philippine Islands, and for other purposes." In its report to the Senate, the Senate Committee on the Philippines, referring to the friar land sections of the bill, characterized the acquisition of the friar lands and their transference to the occupants and holders as a thing that was universally and earnestly desired by the people of the Philippines. This, the report declared, was the sole purpose of those sections dealing with these lands.[2] The report of the House Com-

[1] *Report of the Chief, Bureau of Insular Affairs* (1905), p. 26. For an account of the later phases of the negotiations, see *Report of the Philippine Commission* (1903), pt. i, pp. 38-46 and the Commission's report for 1914, p. 17. Approval of Mr. Taft's work in these negotiations was expressed by Judge Blount, a severe critic of the Taft policies, in his book, *The American Occupation of the Philippines* (New York, 1912), p. 563. See, also, Chamberlin, *The Philippine Problem* (Boston, 1913), pp. 103-112.

[2] *S. Report* 915, 57th Cong., 1st Sess.

mittee on Insular Affairs, after commenting on the hostility of the Filipinos to the friars, disclaimed any desire to pass judgment on the merits of the controversy. "It is sufficient," the report went on, "for the purpose of the proposed legislation that the animosity exists; that it is deep seated and widespread; that it has heretofore resulted in uprisings of the Filipino people, in boodshed and civil war, and that it still is an element dangerous to the peace and prosperity of the islands." [1]

The law authorizing the purchase of the friar lands is comprised in Sections 63, 64, and 65 of the Act of July 1, 1902. Section 63 gave the Philippine government authority to "acquire real estate for public uses by the exercise of the right of eminent domain." Section 64 permitted the exercise of that right in the case of the property of religious orders and others when such property was held in such large tracts and "in such manner as in the opinion of the Commission injuriously to affect the peace and welfare of the people of the Philippine Islands." At the same time the Philippine government was authorized to issue bonds for the purchase, which were to be entirely exempt from taxation in both the Philippines and the United States. Section 65 provided that the lands so acquired were to become a "part and portion of the public property of the government of the Philippine Islands" and "could be held, sold, conveyed, or leased temporarily . . . . on such terms and conditions as it may prescribe, subject to the limitations and conditions provided for in this Act." Further on in the section, actual settlers and occupants were granted a preference to lease, purchase, or acquire their holdings.[2]

This last section relating to the friar lands was destined

[1] *H. Report* 2496, 57th Cong., 1st Sess.

[2] For the text of the law, see 32 *U. S. Stat. L.* 691.

to occasion no little trouble and confusion among legal minds. It incorporated the purchased lands into the public property of the Philippine government and authorized that government to dispose of them at its discretion, "subject to the limitations and conditions provided for" in the Act. The question was whether or not the limitations in the other parts of the Act, particularly the maximum limits of 16 hectares to a person and 1024 hectares to a corporation found in Section 15 applied in disposing of the friar lands.

Precisely such a legal riddle arose in the course of the administration by the Department of the Interior of the Philippine government of these estates. That Department adopted as its policy the sale of the estates in such manner and at such prices as fully to reimburse the government for the expenditures that had been made. It was a comparatively simple problem to carry out this policy in those estates which were already occupied by tenants. There were, however, three estates that were almost wholly unoccupied and represented a heavy drain on the revenues of the government. One of these unoccupied tracts happened to be the San Jose estate in Mondoro and around that tract of land of 22,484 hectares raged a storm of discussion which culminated in a Congressional investigation conducted by the Committee on Insular Affairs of the House of Representatives.[1]

In the course of the investigation, these facts with regard to the San Jose estate transaction, which was the center of controversy, were developed:[2]

[1] For the record of the investigation, see *H. Report* 2289, 61st Cong., 3rd Sess.

[2] For a defense of the administration policy, see C. B. Elliot, *The Philippines to the End of the Commission Government*, pp. 37-58. For adverse criticism, see H. P. Willis, *Our Philippine Problem*, pp. 192-225.

The total area of the friar lands purchased by the government was 400,000 acres in round numbers. Of this, about one-half was occupied and cultivated by nearly 161,000 tenants and the other half constituted the unoccupied, uncultivated, and, consequently, unproductive portion. A large part of these unoccupied lands was represented by the Isabela and San Jose estates. The government realized that, to dispose of these tracts of land within a reasonable time, inducements would have to be offered and that it would be impossible to wait for small holders gradually to take up the estate. At this juncture, a solution of the difficulty appeared in the person of Mr. E. L. Poole, who offered to purchase the entire San Jose estate. Immediately, the legal question arose as to the power of the Philippine government to dispose of the friar lands in parcels of more than 16 hectares to one person, thus posing the query whether or not the limitations of Section 15 of the Organic Act of July 1, 1902 were included in the limitations mentioned in Section 65. The answer hinged on that phrase in the latter section, "subject to the limitations and conditions provided for in this Act." Did Congress mean the limitations and conditions provided for throughout this Act or simply the limitations and conditions in that particular section of the Act? On one side seemed to be the advantage of a natural and usual interpretation of fairly unambiguous language. On the other, it was contended that Congress by conceding a preferential right to occupants to acquire their friar land holdings in this very same section of the Act clearly recognized the fact that the limitations in Section 15 were not to be deemed applicable to the friar-lands sections of the Act. Be that as it may, the question was settled by a decision of theAttorney-general of the United States, handed down December 18, 1909 holding the restrictions found in Section 12, 13, 14, 15 and

16 of the Act to be specific and applicable only to the lands acquired by the treaty of peace with Spain.[1] With the legal clouds dispelled by these decisions, the sale to Mr. E. L. Poole was finally consummated on Nocember 23, 1909.[2] On March 9, 1910 Mr. Poole "executed a deed of trust, setting forth that, in making the purchase, he was acting as the agent of Horace Havemeyer, Charles J. Welch, and Charles H. Senff."[3] At the time of the purchase, Mr. Havemeyer, was a director in the American Sugar Refining Co., but he severed his connection with that company on January 1, 1911. Mr. Welch was a sugar merchant and producer, and Mr. Senff, a retired business man, had once been Vice-President of the American Sugar Refining Co. These three men as individuals were the owners of the San Jose estate. They organized the "Mindoro Development Co.," a corporation chartered in New Jersey, with a very extensive scope of action for the purpose of building a sugar central on that part of the estate comprising 200 acres which the Philippine government, in pursuance to the agreement with Mr. Poole, conveyed to the corporation. In addition, Mr. Welch was instrumental in creating three California agricultural corporations, which bought public lands from the Philippine government in the regions contiguous to the San Jose estate.[4]

In justification of the administrative policy of the Interior Department of the Philippine government, Secretary Worcester presented, with much force, the financial burden on the Filipino people entailed by the non-disposal of the

[1] *H. Doc.* 1071, 61st Cong., 3rd Sess.

[2] *H. Doc.* 1071, 61st Cong., 3rd Sess., p. 2.

[3] *H. Report* 2289, 61st Cong., 3rd Sess., p. 7.

[4] For these details see the Report on the investigation by the House Committee on Insular Affairs, March, 1911, 61st Cong., 3rd Sess., *Report* no. 2289.

unoccupied estates, the increase in wages for Philippine labor, the object lesson that would be furnished in the use of machinery and the most modern methods of cultivation, and the resulting economic well-being due to these things. He, together with Representative Douglas of the Committee on Insular Affairs and Governor General Forbes, hinted that the furore which had been created by the sale of the San Jose estate was an incident that was not entirely distasteful to the beet sugar interests.[1]

During this controversy the people of the Philippines had been by no means uninterested spectators. Their Resident Commissioner, testifying before the House Committee, stated that the grounds for Filipino opposition were twofold. The Filipinos were opposed to the creation of huge estates. They were, also, unable to countenance developmnts which might turn out to be obstacles to the granting of Philippine Independence.[2] And on December 6, 1910, the Philippine Assembly passed Assembly Res. No. 14, "declaring the sale of large and unlimited tracts of land belonging to the so-called 'frair estates' to be contrary to the will, the sentiments, and the interests of the Philippine People."[3]

Franchises

THE SPOONER AMENDMENT

Authorization for granting franchises and the disposal of public lands were the reasons for the introduction of the Spooner Amendment to the Army Appropriation Act of March, 1902. But, as has already beeen said, the modifications forced on the measure by its opponents practically nullified that which had been sought to be conceded.[4]

[1] *H. Report* 2289, 61st Cong., 3rd Sess., pp. 533, 925-941, 1766.

[2] *Ibid.*, pp. 940-997.

[3] *H. Doc.* 1326, 61st Cong., 3rd Sess.

[4] *Supra*, pp. 139-144.

THE ACT OF JULY 1, 1902

Not until the passage of the Organic Act of 1902 did the Philippine government obtain general authority, with certain restrictions, to grant franchises. Section 74 of the Act gave authority for franchise grants with the provisos that no private property should be taken without just compensation or unless its use was actually necessary for the franchise grant; that such grants should be subject to alterations by Congress; that the lands and the rights therein should revert to the government granting the franchise upon its termination or repeal; that stocks and bonds should be issued only in exchange for actual cash or property equivalent to the par value of the stock; that no stock or bond dividends should be issued; that provision should be made in the case of public-service corporations for the regulation of charges, the inspection of books and accounts, and the payment of a percentage of the gross earnings; and that no slave labor should be employed. Section 75 contained stringent restrictions on the real-estate holdings of corporations.[1] By the last paragraph of Section 4 of the Act of February 6, 1905,[2] the provisions of Section 74 of the Act of July 1, 1902 insofar as they were not in conflict with the former were made applicable to corporations the interest on whose bonds might be guaranteed by the Philippine government.

THE PHILIPPINE AUTONOMY ACT OF AUGUST 29, 1916

Section 74 of the Act of July 1, 1902 was superseded by Section 28 of the Philippine Autonomy Act of August 29, 1916.[3] No material changes were involved.

[1] 32 *U. S. Stat. L.*, 691.

[2] *Public*, no. 43, 33 *U. S. Stat. L.*, 689.

[3] *Public*, no. 240, 39 *U. S. Stat. L.*, 545.

Explaining the policy behind the franchise provisions of the Act of July 1, 1902, the Senate Committee on the Philippines said:

> The two sections following these [the public debt sections] relate to the granting of franchises in the islands. The committee feel that it is of the greatest importance for the proper development of the islands that capital be encouraged to enter the islands, but in order to prevent any improper exploitation which would be to the detriment of the inhabitants these sections are strongly guarded. . . . [1]

The report of the House Committee on Insular Affairs expressed the belief that the sections relating to franchises thoroughly safeguarded the islands from "corporate or private greed" and at the same time offered "inviting opportunity for legitimate business investment." [2]

And in his remarks on the bill, Senator Lodge alluded to the clauses providing for franchises. He said they were guarded with the "utmost care" and "in every possible way" compatible with the need of offering sufficient inducements to attract capital to the islands.[3]

Public Debt

That the state of a nation's credit is a very important factor in governmental finance is a sufficiently obvious truism. Control, therefore, of a country's borrowing capacity and the manner of its exercise is certainly not an inconsiderable power. How Congress has tried to lay out with an almost mathematical precision the metes and bounds of the borrowing power of the Philippine government will be the theme of the succeeding paragraphs in this chapter.

[1] *S. Report* 915, 57th Cong., 1st Sess.

[2] *H. Report* 2496, 57th Cong., 1st Sess.

[3] *Cong. Record*, 57th Cong., 1st Sess., p. 5031.

THE ACT OF JULY 1, 1902

The first bond issue provided for by an act of Congress was the one which was authorized by Section 64 of the Act of July 1, 1902 for the purpose of financing the purchase of the friar lands. These bonds were exempted from taxation by the Philippine and American governments or any local governments in either country. This tax exemption feature was for the purpose of making the bonds as attractive as possible. Under Section 66 of the same Act, the Philippine government obtained power to authorize, with the approval of the President of the United States, Phiilppine municipalities to issue bonds when current taxation was inadequate for public improvements. Such indebtedness, however, could not exceed five per cent of the assessed valuation of the real estate of the municipality. These bonds were to bear interest at five per cent and to be exempt from the payment of taxes of the Philippine government or any local authority in the Philippines, or the government of the United States. Unlike then, the friar land bonds, these municipal bonds were not immune from state and local taxation in the United States. Two other sections—68 and 69—contained miscellaneous provisions regarding the use of the funds derived from the sale of such bonds, and sinking fund, etc. Sections 70, 71 and 73 conferred power on the Philippine government to authorize the city of Manila, the approval of the President of the United States being first had, to incur indebtedness not to exceed four million dollars for the construction of sewerage and water supply systems.

THE ACT OF FEBRUARY 6, 1905

By the first section of the Act of February 6, 1905 all Philippine government bonds were exempted from all taxation either in the Philippines or the United States. The second section authorized the central government of the Philippines, to issue bonds, with the approval of the President, for port and harbor works, bridges, roads, public buildings, and other public improvements. A maximum limit of five million dollars was provided. Section 3 related to municipal bonds, and Section 4 empowered the Philippine government to guarantee, under certain conditions, interest up to four per cent per annum on bonds issued by any railroad company undertaking the construction of railway lines in the Philippines.[1]

CONGRESSIONAL COMMENT ON THE ACTS OF 1902 AND 1905

During the discussion in the Senate of the bill which finally became the law of July 1, 1902, several opposition Senators voiced objections to the public debt provision of the bill. Senator Dubois criticised the authorization of the issuance of bonds for public improvements in municipalities because it would not be the Filipinos who would decide whether or not it would be wise to issue bonds for such improvements.[2] Senator Clay, of Georgia attacked the vesting of vast powers in the hands of the Philippine Commission.[3] The reasons for the affirmative were clearly presented in the committee reports in the Senate and House urging the passage of the bill.[4] In his remarks in the Senate, Mr. Lodge declared that the reason why the frairland bonds had a wider tax exemption feature than the municipal bonds was because the committee did not desire to encourage municipal indebtedness.[5]

[1] *Public*, no. 43, 33 *U. S. Stat. L.* 689.

[2] *Cong. Record*, 57th Cong., 1st Sess., p. 5851.

[3] *Ibid.*, p. 6100.

[4] *S. Report* 915 and *H. Report* 2496, 57th Cong., 1st Sess.

[5] *Cong. Record*, 57th Cong., 1st Sess., pp. 7737-7738.

In the discussion of the Act of 1906, Senator Newlands emphasized the view that the United States created some sort of an obligation on its part and that, thereby, its interest became "deeply and essentially concerned." [1] Replying to these remarks of Mr. Newlands, Senator Lodge authoritatively stated the policy with respect to these bonds. He said it had never been America's policy to guarantee them. Rather, it was to give the Philippines as much freedom of action as possible and to have the bonds stand on their own merits. True enough, the United States had exempted those bonds from taxation within her own territory. But as Senator Lodge remarked: "It seems to me that to enable the people in those islands to borrow the necessary money for municipal improvements at the lowest possible rate, where it can be done without any serious loss to us—in fact, with no loss at all—that will be susceptible, and without involving the United States in any way, is sensible and advisable legislation. . . ." [2]

THE ACT OF AUGUST 29, 1916

Section 11 of the Act of August 29, 1916, commonly known as the "Jones" or "Autonomy" Act, increased the limit of Philippine indebtedness to $15,000,000 exclusive of the friar land bonds, while the limit on bonds issued by provinces and municipalities was placed at seven per cent of the aggregate tax valuation of their property.

THE ACT OF JULY 21, 1921

Two reasons, one permanent and the other temporary, combined to render necessary the passage of an act to increase the bonded indebtedness in 1921. The efforts to

[1] *Cong. Record*, 58th Cong., 3rd Sess., p. 134.

[2] *Cong. Record*, 58th Cong., 3rd Sess., pp. 134-135, 343.

induce outside capital to enter the Philippines had not been productive of results. Consequently, the Philippine government embarked on far-reaching schemes to infuse a quickened vitality into the economic development of the country. Extensive loans were granted for sugar centrals and vegetable oil mills. The national cement, coal, and other companies were organized and financed by the government. A government bank, known as the Philippine National Bank, was chartered and through it these loans were negotiated. Soon after the signing of the armistice in 1918 the crash came. Inflated prices fell with a thud. The demand for Philippine products suddenly halted. Under these conditions, the Bank had to suffer losses on its loans. The government whose money was in the bank, in turn, found itself in serious financial difficulties.

To remedy the situation, a bill[1] was introduced at the first session of the Sixty-Seventh Congress. As introduced, it provided for increasing the indebtedness limit from $15,000,000 to $30,000,000. The provinces and municipalities still had the seven per cent limit. In addition, however, it was proposed that in computing the indebtedness of the central government those bonds of a valuation not to exceed $10,000,000 which the central government might issue and which were secured by an equivalent amount of provincial and municipal bonds should not be counted.

In favorably reporting the bill, the House Committee on Insular Affairs declared that the increase was conservative and one that was " urgently needed to meet the steady progress in the development of the islands." Speaking of the Philippine government's effort to encourage agriculture and industry, the Committee said that process had resulted in " tying up the funds of the government " in forms which

[1] *H. R.* 5756.

made "such funds temporarily unavailable to meet the demands of the public."[1] When the bill reached the Senate, the Committee on Territories and Insular Possessions amended it so as to authorize an increase by $10,000,000 of the amount of certificates of indebtedness which the Philippine government could issue under the Currency Act of March 2, 1903. With this amendment, the Senate Committee favorably reported the bill, using much the same arguments as those that had been presented in the House.[2]

Representative Towner urged the passage of the bill in the House in these words:

> . . . the extension which is asked for in this bill would be perfectly justified merely in the ordinary course, because the business of the Philippine Islands, the progress and development of their commercial interests, the increase of the wealth of the islands, would make $15,000,000 as a limitation altogether too small an amount. Conditions, however, warrant action outside of those considerations. . . .[3]

While the bill was pending before the House, hearings were held by the Committee on Insular Affairs. Testifying before the Committee, General McIntyre, the chief of the Bureau of Insular Affairs, stated that a further indebtedness was necessary to carry out the plan of public works in the islands and to construct public buildings. That need, he asserted, had been recognized for a long time. But, he went on,

> we ask for it particularly at this time because of an emergency in the currency situation in the Philippine Islands. That is, the gold fund in the United States, of the Philippine govern-

[1] *H. Report* 55, 67th Cong., 1st Sess.

[2] *S. Report* 181, 67th Cong., 1st Sess.

[3] *Cong. Record*, 67th Cong., 1st Sess., p. 2767.

ment, has been exhausted once or twice within the last year, and from the proceeds of these bonds we hope to establish a sufficient gold fund in the United States against which exchange can be sold in the islands.[1]

Apropos of these remarks of General McIntyre, Mr. Towner, the Chairman of the Committee interposed with the following:

Now it is a very significant fact that during the first three months of the year 1921 these purchases by the Philippines from the United States have fallen off very greatly compared with the preceding years, largely on account of the conditions that have been detailed by General McIntyre, and also very largely on account of the exchange situation. . . .

The United States, of course, is tremendously interested in the Philippines, outside of any fact that they are a part of the United States, because of the growing business and the desire of the Philippine Islanders to purchase their supplies of the United States, and we have an immediate interest in seeing that financial conditions in the Philippine Islands are stabilized, for selfish reasons as well as the fact that we are certainly under some obligations to them as long as they remain a part of our territory.[2]

The bill obtained the signature of the President on July 21, 1921.[3]

THE ACT OF MAY 31, 1922

On February 15, 1922 a bill (H. R. 10442) was introduced to extend further the limit of indebtedness of the Philippine government. It authorized a maximum indebtedness for the central government, exclusive of the friar

[1] *Hearings*, Committee on Insular Affairs, May 2, 1921, pp. 4-6.

[2] *Ibid.*, p. 7.

[3] See *Public*, no. 42.

land bonds, of a sum equivalent to 10 per cent of the aggregate tax valuation of its property and provided the same limitation for the city of Manila. The provinces and municipalities of the Archipelago were restricted to 7 per cent of the tax valuation of their property. In computing the indebtedness of the government, those bonds, not exceeding $10,000,000 which that government might issue and which were secured by an equivalent amount of bonds by the provincial and municipal governments were not to be counted.[1]

The same reasons were operative in the case of this last extension of the limit of indebtedness of the Philippines as had obtained in the preceding instance during the passage of the Act of July 21, 1921. Government funds continued to be tied up in frozen assets; and the exchange value of Philippine currency in the American market sorely needed bolstering in order to keep up Philippine-American trade.[2]

The picture presented by this series of laws on agricultural, timber, and mining lands, including that novel adventure in the purchase of the friar lands, and the legislation on franchises and the public debt can be best described as one completely colored with excessive caution. Such solicitude for the public lands, for the friar lands, for the mines, the forests, the franchises, and the public debts arose more out of conditions in American history and politics than from an objective examination of Philippine needs and problems. In the legislation for public lands the model, and an excellent model it was, became the homestead legislation of America. But the severe outlines of the model were slightly marred by several conflicting influences. The

[1] See *Public*, no. 228, passed May 31, 1922.

[2] See the statement of Gen. McIntyre before the House Committee on Insular Affairs, *Hearings*, February 21, March 7, 22, 1922, p. 6 and also *H. Report* 874 and *Senate Report*, 718, 67th Cong., 2nd Sess.

solons from the South listened to a voice from the past and, with vivid memories of the horrors of the reconstruction period, strove for restrictions and yet more restrictions to prevent exploitation. A more modern and pragmatic view was that of the beet sugar interests, which, in the judgment of persons in authoritative positions, were friendly to, if not partly responsible for, the restrictions in the Public Land Act of 1902.[1] Nor need we wander far to locate the origin of so much Congressional prescience anent franchises and the practices connected with them. Students of state and municipal government will, also, readily discern the source of so much Congressional severity as is expressed in the restrictions on the use of the public credit and the limitations on the amount of the public debt.

[1] See the views of Representative Douglas, Governor Forbes and Secretary Worcester in *H. Report* 2289, 61st Cong., 3rd Sess., on pp. 925-941, 1066 and 533.

CHAPTER VIII

Currency Legislation

At the time of the American occupation of the Philippines there were five kinds of currency in circulation: the Mexican pesos, the Spanish-Filipino coins specially provided by Spain for circulation in the Philippine Islands, half pesos and subsidiary coinage of various kinds, a miscellaneous collection of early Spanish pesos and fractional coins, together with the coins of the neighboring countries, and several million pesos of paper currency issued by the Spanish-Filipino Bank of Manila. All of these coins were of silver and varied in weight and fineness.[1]

All of them circulated, normally, at par with each other and at a value higher than their bullion value. This was due, of course, to the fact that the supply of the money being limited, they circulated at their scarcity value and one that was greater than the bullion value of the dearest, which was the Mexican peso. An estimate made by the Secretary of Finance and Justice of the Philippine Government in 1915 placed the total amount of these silver coins in circulation in 1903 at Pfs. 34,098,901.69 and the notes of the Spanish-Filipino Bank in circulation at Pfs. 2,057,000.[2]

To this multiplicity of coins were added the different denominations of American currency after the American occu-

[1] Kemmerer, *Modern Currency Reforms* (New York, 1916), pp. 249-250.

[2] *Report of the Philippine Commission* (1915), pp. 191-192; for a much higher estimate of the amount of the outstanding bank notes see Kemmerer, *ibid.*, p. 250. Pfs. is the abbreviation used to designate the Philippine press prior to American occupation.

pation. For the payment of troops and the purchase of supplies the American Government sent American money into the islands and, consequently, some sort of an exchange value had to be established between the dollar based on the gold standard and these silver coins existing in the Archipelago at the time.

Until the coming into effect of the Currency Act of March 2, 1903 the Philippine Government tried to hold the local currency at a gold value of $0.50 to the peso or at a rate of 2 to 1. In this undertaking the Military Government, at first, and, later, its successor, the Civil Government, encountered numerous difficulties due to the depreciation of silver in relation to gold. The Government authorities found it impossible to maintain the original ratio for any considerable length of time and continually had to adjust the ratio to correspond with the changing market value of silver.

Because of this instability, the foreign trade of the country was hampered and the Government met with difficulties with which, otherwise, it would not have had to deal. More specifically, the silver standard interfered with the Governments' finances by occasioning financial losses, causing uncertainties in the budget, and creating unusual accounting difficulties. While there was a loud clamor from the importers and exporters for currency reform, yet it is probably true that the main impulse for the currency reform movement came from the difficulties created for the government by the chaotic state of Philippine currencies at the time.[1]

[1] See on this point, Kemmerer, *op. cit.*, p. 281. On pp. 267-300, he discusses the efforts made by the Philippine Government to establish some sort of a stable ratio between gold and silver currency.

PROPOSED REFORMS

Public discussion of currency reform ran along three different channels. There were those who wanted the re-coining of the Mexican and the Spanish-Filipino coins and the maintenance of the silver standard. Leading export merchants and bankers of Manila were warm partisans of this proposal. Others wanted the introduction of the United States currency system into the Philippines not only to stabilize Philippine money but also as a part of the political policy of the Government. The third group desired the adoption of the gold standard with a new coinage with a peso as a unit which would be equivalent to half the American dollar.[1]

THE GOLD EXCHANGE STANDARD PLAN

The plan for a distinctive Philippine coinage on a gold basis was the one that gained increasing support as time went on. It was first advanced in the Report of the United States Philippine Commission dated January 24, 1901.[2] In 1901 the War Department sent Mr. C. A. Conant to the Philippines to investigate and make recommendations on the currency situation. On November 25, 1901, he made his report to the Secretary of War and recommended the gold-exchange standard system for the Philippines.[3]

[1] For an examination of the history and merits of these three alternatives see Kemmerer, *op. cit.*, pp. 300-313; see also, Willis, *Our Philippine Problem*, pp. 307-309.

[2] Pp. 91-92.

[3] C. A. Conant, *Special Report on Coinage and Banking in the Philippine Islands*, 1901; other early reports on this subject are: *Report of the Philippine Commission*, 1900; E. M. Harden, *Report on Financial and Industrial Conditions in the Philippine Islands* (Washington, 1898); and C. R. Edwards, *Memorandum on Currency and Exchange in the Philippine Islands* (Washington, 1900).

The main points in the currency system which Mr. Conant recommended were:

First, the creation of a distinctive silver coin for the Philippines which should be legal tender for fifty cents in the gold money of the United States.

Second, the division of this silver unit coin, to be known as the peso, into one hundred equal parts called centavos.

Third, the issuance by the government of the Philippine Islands of these coins in quantities sufficient only to meet the necessary requirements of commerce.

Fourth, the maintenance of the parity of the new coins with gold through the limitation of the amount in circulation and the establishment of the gold reserve to be employed, in the discretion of the government, for the direct exchange of silver for gold, and in such other ways as it may think necessary to maintain the parity fixed by law.

Fifth, the withdrawal of the legal tender quality from all kinds of currency except the new silver coins and the gold money of the United States after specified dates.[1]

THE ACT OF JULY 1, 1902

The first serious efforts to obtain congressional action on the subject of currency reform for the Philippines came with the consideration of the civil government bill which became law in July, 1902. After hearings had been held on the subject by both the Senate Committee on the Philippines and the House Committee on Insular Affairs serious

[1] C. A. Conant, "The Currency of the Philippine Islands," in *Annals of the American Academy of Political and Social Science*, November, 1902; see also the *Report* on the introduction of the gold exchange standard into China and other silver-using countries by the Commission on International Exchange, published as *House Document* 144, 58th Cong., 2nd Sess. and the report by Professor Jenks to the Secretary of War in 1902 on *Certain Economic Questions in the English and Dutch Colonies in the orient.*

differences of opinion arose between the two houses. The House committee favorably reported the Philippine Commission plan [1] for which the Senate Committee later substituted a silver standard plan. Failure on the part of the conferees of both houses to reach an agreement resulted in the postponement of thoroughgoing currency reform and the adoption, as a part of the Act of July 1, 1902, of items authorizing the Philippine Government to issue subsidiary silver coins.[2]

THE CURRENCY ACT OF 1903

In the year 1903 a bill was introduced in the House of Representatives to establish a standard of value and to provide a coinage system for the Philippine Islands.[3] The committee report recommending passage of the bill mentioned two aims that the bill sought to accomplish: To stabilize the value of Philippine money in relation to the gold exchange standard and to disturb as little as possible the then existing coinage system of the Philippine Islands.[4] In the debates in the House the Democrats who were in the minority solidly opposed the proposed legislation and favored the speedy introduction of the American system of currency. They were aided in their opposition to the bill reported by the Committee on Insular Affairs by several leading Republican members of the House Committee on Banking and Currency, among them being Mr. Hill of Connecticut, the chairman of the committee.[5] The opponents of

[1] *House Report* no. 2496, 57th Cong., 1st Sess.

[2] See secs. 77-79 of the Act of July 1, 1902, in 32 *U. S. Stat. L.*, 710-711; on the influence of the silver interests on the action of the Senate, see Willis, *Our Philippine Problem*, p. 303.

[3] *H. R.* 15520, 57th Cong., 2nd Sess.

[4] *House Reports* no. 3023 and 3834, 57th Cong., 2nd Sess.

[5] *Cong. Record*, 57th Cong., 2nd Sess., p. 1048 *et seq.*

the bill reproached the majority for their lack of fidelity to the gold standard, mentioned the political and trade advantages flowing from the introduction of the American currency system, and minimized the supposed difficulties that would flow from such a solution of the problem.

Thus Mr. Williams of Mississippi was for the extension of the American coinage system because, even if America left the Islands, that system would be "a stimulating agency for the expansion of American trade." [1]

On the other hand, the Chairman of the House Committee on Insular Affairs and those who supported him relied mainly on the opinions of the higher officials of the Philippine government and of those experts who had, previously, been sent to the Far East on missions of investigation. Mr. Cooper declared that the system would be the same as that which was then in working operation in India and Java. He referred with approval to the report of the Taft Philippine Commission in 1900 and to the testimony of Governor Taft himself before the Committee on Insular Affairs in 1902 strongly advocating the bill which he (Mr. Cooper) was sponsoring. The chief objection to the adoption of American money lay in the fact that it would occasion a great disturbance in wages, prices and in commerce and industry.[2] Moreover, the difference between the bullion and face values of the silver coin which would be the equivalent of the American dollar, if the proposition of the minority was adopted, would be so great that it would be a strong inducement to counterfeiting.[3]

Another majority member of the Committee on Insular Affairs said:

[1] *Cong. Record*, 57th Cong., 2nd Sess., p. 1074.

[2] *Cong. Record*, 57th Cong., 2nd Sess., p. 1020.

[3] *Ibid.*, p. 1039.

The idea that occupied the minds of many members of our committee when we began the investigation of the question was that of Americanism in the Philippine Islands, regardless of any industrial or commercial conditions. It was our belief . . . that the introduction of American coinage in denomination and in nomenclature would tend to Americanize the Philippine Islands.

In spite of these prepossessions of the committee members, those belonging to the majority party had come to the conclusion that the introduction of American money would be unwise. "In doing so," he (Mr. Tawney) continued, "we believed, as did the Commissioners and Governor Taft, that it was not only justice to the people of the Islands, but it would tend to conciliate the natives of the Archipelago more than any one thing the government could do." [1]

With the powerful aid of their temporary allies on the Republican side, the Democrats in the House succeeded by a vote of 147 to 127 in substituting their amendment for the committee bill.[2]

In contrast with its attitude during the preceding session, the Senate now took the bill in charge, struck off the provisions put in by the Democrats in the House, and inserted in their stead the original sections of the House bill. In addition, the Senate approved an amendment providing for an international conference on the subject of establishing a fixed commercial exchange ratio between the currencies of the gold and silver standard countries.[3]

When the measure reached the House again, the Committee on Insular Affairs promptly recommended passage of the Senate bill with only minor amendments. The two or

[1] *Cong. Record*, 57th Cong., 2nd Sess., p. 1081.

[2] *Ibid.*, p. 1084.

[3] *Ibid.*, p. 2248.

three leaders of the revolt on the Republican side became frightened by the threatened renewal of the silver agitation and agreed to reverse their votes.

Mr. Hill, the severest critic of the bill, explained his changed attitude thus:

> . . . I stand here first, last, and all the time against any renewal of any attempt to go through the miserable farce that we played from 1892 to 1898 on the silver question. I believe in killing this snake while he is young and not waiting until he is full grown and have another tussle with him as we did in 1896. For that reason I reserve my own freedom of individual action on this question today.[1]

Elimination of the Senate amendment for an international conference removed all points of disagreement between the two Houses and the bill finally became a law on March 2, 1903.[2] The Act established a theoretical unit of value known as the gold peso equivalent to half the value of the American dollar. Another section authorized the coinage of silver pesos which were to be maintained at a parity with the theoretical gold peso. To maintain this parity the Philippine government was given power to issue temporary certificates of indebtedness not to exceed $10,000,000 at any one time. Other sections empowered the Philippine government to issue silver certificates for silver pesos, made the silver peso legal tender for the payment of debts, and vested authority in the insular government to create and maintain the gold exchange standard system.

LOCAL CURRENCY LEGISLATION IN THE PHILIPPINES

On October 10, 1903, the Philippine Commission passed the Gold Standard Act designed to place the new currency

[1] *Ibid.*, p. 2575.

[2] *Public*, no. 137, 32 *U. S. Stat. L.* 952.

system on a working basis.[1] To maintain the parity of the silver Philippine peso with the theoretical gold-standard peso, the Act created a gold standard fund from sales of certificates of indebtedness authorized by the Act of March 2, 1903, profits of seigniorage, profits from the sale of exchange and other profits arising from the governmental function of creating and maintaining a stable system of currency. This gold standard fund was to be a separate and trust fund. Part of the fund would be kept in Manila and part in the government depositaries in the United States.

To maintain the gold standard value of the Philippine peso the treasurer of the Philippine Islands was authorized:

(1) To exchange drafts on the gold standard fund, the premium charged to be fixed by law.

(2) To exchange at par United States paper currency for Philippine currency and *vice versa* with the approval of the Secretary of Finance and Justice.

(3) To exchange, on like approval, United States gold coin or gold bars for Philppine currency, the premium charged representing only the expenses of transportation.

(4) To withdraw from circulation Philippine currency exchanged and deposited in the treasury except in response to similar counter-demands or to increase the circulation.

(5) To withdraw from circulation United States money exchanged for Philippine currency except in the contingencies mentioned in the preceding paragraph.

The Philippine Commission Act also authorized the treasurer to exchange Philippine pesos on demand for subsidiary coins and subsidary coins for Philippine pesos.

The silver coins received in exchange for silver certificates were to constitute also a trust fund to be used only for the redemption of such certificates.

[1] Act 938.

These two fundamental laws of the Philippine currency system illustrate very clearly the theory underlying it. Its basic premises are a limited coinage and the fixation of a stable ratio between gold and silver coins through the complete assurance of exchangeability of gold with silver at the ratio fixed by law. The maintainance of a fixed value for the silver coins in relation to gold depends upon the ability of the government to meet all demands for the exchange of American currency for Philippine currency or *vice versa* either in the Philippines or the United States, charging therefor a premium equal to the expenses that would be incurred if a similar amount of metal were to be actually transported. The theory assumes that if the balance in Philippine-American trade should happen to be against the Philippines, the difference would, under ordinary conditions, be covered by the export of gold from the Islands to the United States. Under the gold exchange standard system, however, business houses with accounts to settle in the United States, would purchase drafts from the Philippine government on the gold standard fund in New York and such drafts would be used for the settlement of those accounts. The government of the Philippines withdraws from circulation the money paid for drafts on the other country, and this creates a corresponding scarcity of monetary circulation. Money, if the outward flow continues, the theory holds, becomes relatively scarce and sooner or later a point is reached where, because of the very scarcity of money, a reverse change in the balance of trade is accomplished.[1]

THE WITHDRAWAL OF LOCAL CURRENCY

Before going into the later changes in the Philippine currency laws, it might be well to glance at the means adopted to substitute the new currency for the old coins on January

[1] See Kemmerer, *op. cit.*, pp. 314-323.

1, 1904.[1] On October 23, 1903 the Civil Governor issued a proclamation providing that Mexican dollars would not be received for public dues after the first day of the new year.[2] By executive order of the civil Governor in May and July of 1903, payments for government supplies and in settlement of government contracts were to be made in the new currency.[3] On December 28, an Act was passed providing for the payment of taxes, fees, fines, penalties, government salaries and other public charges in the new currency.[4] Importation of local currency into the Islands came under a legal ban by the Act of January 14, 1904.[5] On the first day of this same month an Executive order had been issued providing for the receipt and redemption of local currency.[6] But the most drastic of the measures taken was the passage of the Local Currency Taxation Act on January 27, 1904.[7] The Act imposed an ad valorem tax on contracts and other written instruments payable in local currency, upon bank deposits of local currency, and required all merchants doing business in local currency to pay a special license tax.

How effective these measures were is shown by the report of the Secretary of Finance and Justice of the Philippine government for the year 1915. He estimated the silver currency in circulation in 1903 to be Pfs. 34,098,901.69. Of that total only Pfs. 330,000 remained in 1915. In addition there were, in 1903, notes of the Spanish-Filipino bank amounting to Pfs. 2,057,000. To replace these coins withdrawn from circulation, there were, in 1915, 52,913,754.67

[1] See Kemmerer, *op. cit.*, p. 330.

[2] *Report of the Philippine Commission*, 1903, pt. iii, p. 284.

[3] *Executive Orders and Proclamations*, 1903, pp. 47-48, 67, 85.

[4] *Official Gazette*, 1904, p. 17.

[5] Act no. 1042.

[6] *Official Gazette*, 1904, p. 18.

[7] Act no. 1045. *Official Gazette*, 1904, pp. 105-107.

pesos in silver coinage, 31,113,220 pesos in silver certificates and 5,327,492.50 pesos in notes of the Bank of the Philippine Islands.[1]

THE ACT OF FEBRUARY 6, 1905

After the passage of the Currency Act of March 2, 1903 the next congressional legislation on Philippine currency came in 1905. The most important provision of the Act of February 6 of that year was the section designed to induce foreign capital to invest in the construction of railway lines in the islands. The law authorized the Philippine government to guarantee, under certain conditions, the interest on bonds which the railway companies might issue for financing construction work. It is under the provisions of this legislation that the "Philippine Railway Co." and the "Manila Railroad Co." have been operating. Of these two corporations, the property of the second has been bought by the Philippine government, and the first still manages, with varying success, to maintain itself as a going concern. On the whole, it can be said that the results of the railway provisions of the Act have been far from satisfactory.

The part of the Act dealing with currency simply authorized the issuance of silver certificates to a maximum denomination of five hundred pesos instead of ten pesos as before.[2]

In 1906 the continued rise in the price of silver threatened to create a situation where the bullion value of the Philippine silver peso would be higher than its token value. To meet this difficulty a bill[3] was introduced authorizing

[1] *Report of the Philippine Commission*, 1915, pp. 191-192. For a much fuller account of the steps taken for the withdrawal of the old currency, see Kemmerer, *op. cit.*, pp. 324-346.

[2] *Public*, no. 43, 33 *U. S. Stat. L.*, 697.

[3] S. 6243.

the Philippine Commission, with the approval of the President, to change the weight and fineness of the Philippine peso. It also authorized the use of gold coin in the treasury certificate reserve fund to a maximum of sixty per cent of the total outstanding certificates. The bill became a law on June 23, 1906.[1]

The gold standard fund which was established by the Philippine Commission Gold Standard Act of October 10, 1903 had, by 1911, risen to 43 per cent of the entire circulation.[2] In that year the Philippine legislature determined on 35 per cent of the money in circulation and available for circulation as the size of the Gold Standard Fund and transferred the excess funds to the general fund of the treasury. Half of the fund, however, could be loaned to municipalities and to the Manila Railroad Co. for the extension of its lines. The treasury certificate fund was to remain equal to the silver certificates in circulation.[3] By subsequent laws in 1915 the amount made available for long-term investment was increased to 80 per cent of the Gold Standard Fund.[4] Of these changes the Secretary of Finance in 1915 said:

> This latter amount [20 per cent] under careful administration would be sufficient to carry on the ordinary exchange operations which are a factor of importance in the maintainance of the parity of the currency with gold, but would not be sufficient to maintain confidence in our currency system or to meet emergencies or abnormal conditions should they arise. . . . [5]

[1] *Public*, no. 274, 34 *U. S. Stat. L.*, 453. On this law see the remarks of Representative Cooper in the *Cong. Record*, 59th Cong., 1st Sess. and also the joint letter of C. A. Conant and J. W. Jenks to the Secretary of War dated May, 1906, and published as *Senate Document*, 453, 59th Cong., 1st Sess.

[2] Kemmerer, *op. cit.*, p. 367.

[3] Act of December 8, 1911, known as Act no. 2083.

[4] Acts no. 2344, 2465, 2591, 2592.

[5] *Report of the Philippine Commission*, 1915, p. 191.

In August, 1918, the currency laws were further amended by the Philippine legislature. The Gold Standard Fund and the Treasury Certificates Fund were merged into a Currency Reserve Fund. The amount of the fund was to be equal to the treasury certificates in circulation plus 15 per cent of the coins in circulation or available for circulation.[1]

Further amendments came through the law enacted on January 28, 1921.[2] The Secretary of Finance was empowered to increase or decrease the premium charged on drafts and telegraphic transfers, and the Governor General was authorized, upon the recommendation of the Secretary of Finance, to suspend the sale of exchange. This law, also, fixed the amount of the Currency Reserve Fund at 60 per cent of the treasury certificates in circulation up to a total circulation of 120 million pesos, and 100 per cent of the circulation in excess of 120 million.

These successive depletions of the currency reserve fund did not have any serious consequences on the successful working of the system until the year 1919 when the balance of trade went heavily against the Islands, part of the fund itself being tied up among the non-liquid assets of the Philippine National Bank. These decreases in the currency reserve fund began in 1911 under the Forbes administration with the passage of the laws authorizing the loaning of portions of the fund to municipalities and provinces for the construction of public works and to the Manila Railroad Co. for the extension of its lines. The Philippine National Bank, in investing portions of the fund on long-term loans for the construction of sugar centrals and the like, was thus simply following a policy inaugurated as far back as 1911. To meet the currency difficulties in 1919 the government

[1] Act no. 2776. Act no. 2711, known as the *Administrative Code*, had not made any changes.

[2] Act no. 939, *Official Gazette*, vol. xix, no. 28, p. 601.

raised the rates of exchange until they reached 11 per cent, while the Manila banks charged as high as 16 per cent.[1] In order to bring down the exchange rates to normal and thus remove that serious hindrance to Philippine-American trade. the government of the Philippine Islands passed the Currency Act of 1922 practically placing the system back on the basis of the law in 1904.[2]

By this law of 1922 the treasury certificate fund was restored to 100 per cent of the treasury certificates in circulation and the Gold Standard Fund fixed at 15 per cent of the money in circulation including both coin and treasury certificates. Moreover, the Gold Standard Fund was to be increased until it reached 25 per cent. The law made the two funds again independent of each other.

At the time that the Currency Law of 1922 was passed, the Philippine government had reached the maximum limit placed on its bonded indebtedness by the Autonomy Act of 1916. Additional funds had to be raised if the aims of the Currency Law were to be carried out. Under these circumstances the introduction of bills for raising the limits of bonded indebtedness of the Philippines became necessary, and this was done in 1921.

The passage of this bill [3] gave authority to the Philippine government to increase its bonded indebtedness from $15,000,000 to $30,000,000 and to issue, to an amount not exceeding $10,000,000, certificates of indebtedness in addition to those authorized by the Act of March 2, 1903.[4]

[1] See the article by B. F. Wright, on "The Revised Currency Law of June, 1922" in the *Philippines Herald*, Manila, January 7, 1923.

[2] Act no. 3058, passed June 13, 1922.

[3] *H. R.* 5756, 67th Cong., 1st Sess. The bill became law on July 21, 1921.

[4] For references on *H. R.* 5756 see *H. R. Report* no. 55, and *S. Report* no. 181, 67th Cong., 1st Sess.; *Hearing* before the House Committee on Insular Affairs, May 2, 1921; for the text of the law itself see *Public*, no. 42.

The next year found the currency situation still acute, and during the first months of 1922 the House Committee on Insular Affairs held hearings on the subject of a further extension of the limits of Philippine indebtedness.[1] Testifying before the committee, General McIntyre, the chief of the Bureau of Insular Affairs, said: "The urgent necessity of increasing the limit at this time arises from the fact that the Philippine Government is not in a position to maintain the parity of its currency with the gold standard fixed by law."[2] In accordance with the recommendations of the War Department and the Governor General of the Philippines, a law was passed on May 31, 1922 extending the limit of the bonded indebtedness of the Philippines to 10 per cent of the aggregate tax valuation of its property.[3] This placed the authorized indebtedness around $75,000,000 exclusive of the friar land bonds and the bonds of the provinces and municipalities. Out of this new increase in indebtedness $22,500,000 represented the needs of the currency system.[4]

This currency crisis in 1919-1922 served to draw attention to the fact that the American government morally, at least, stands behind the Philippine currency system. The Bureau of Insular Affairs not only sponsored the increase in the debt limit and arranged the sale of Philippine bonds, but also took an active and dominant part in the reorganization of the affairs and determination of policies of the Philippine National Bank. The Wood-Forbes mission of investigation devoted a great deal of its time to a thorough

[1] *Hearings* before the Committee on Insular Affairs, February 21, 1922, 67th Cong., 2nd Sess.

[2] *Ibid.*, p. 6.

[3] *Public*, no. 228.

[4] See *Hearings* before the Committee on Insular Affairs on *H. R.* 10442, February and March, 1922, 67th Cong., 2nd Sess.; also *H. Report* 874 and *S. Report* 718, 67th Cong., 2nd Sess.

study of the finances of the Philippine government on which depended the successful working of the currency system. And the United States government further aided by using the funds destined for its military forces in the islands to ease the situation in the sale of exchange between the Philippines and the United States.

CHAPTER IX

Conclusion

Of the different phases of economic legislation that have been taken up in these chapters — the tariff, the coastwise laws, public lands, franchises, the public debt and the currency—the first has been the most controversial and instructive. Statutes on public lands, franchises, and the public debt have erred more on the side of severity than laxity. The carefully guarded provisions of the Act of July 1, 1902 on these subjects remained with but slight alterations until the granting of qualified power to the Philippine Legislature to deal with public lands and franchises by virtue of the Act of August 29, 1916. Thus the power to dispose of public lands and franchises was hedged with restrictive safeguards until legislative authority, of a qualified but fairly extensive nature, was transferred to the representatives of the Filipino people. The Congressional conscience proved highly sensitive in the matter of the disposition of public lands, the issuance of bonds, and the bestowal of franchises. That great ogre of American politics—the corporations, oftentimes referred to in more expressive, as well as more forceful phraseology—had not a little to do with creating that sensitiveness. Present, also, were the beet sugar interests, who were not particularly sorry that those restrictions crept in. Thus, at bottom, these laws represented pragmatic conclusions, born of American conditions and political struggles.

On the issue of the tariff relations between the Philippines and the United States, the principle has been to facilitate control of the Philippine market, with an endeavor to grant the Philippines reciprocal concessions provided these contained no menace to American industries. While the law as it stands to-day does not apply in all respects the principle of reciprocity, yet that law represents a measure of substantial justice which took no less than ten years of constant agitation in Congress to accomplish. The Philippine Autonomy Act of 1916 conferred power upon the Philippine Legislature to pass tariff laws applicable to Philippine trade with foreign countries other than the United States. Although control of a country's foreign trade cannot prove of vital moment, if such control extends only to a portion of that trade, nevertheless liberalism has been shown in this case to the extent of such control.

On the other hand, in the matter of coastwise shipping legislation, the Merchant Marine Act of 1920 embodied, in respect of its Philippine section, a distinctly backward step foreshadowing, as it did, the establishment of a monopoly.

A glance at the changes in the foreign trade of the Philippines and the results of other economic legislation mentioned in the preceding chapters may not be without interest. The volume of Philippine foreign trade increased from 62,054,525 pesos in 1895 to 132,017,512 pesos in 1909, 202,171,484 pesos in 1913, 601,124,276 pesos in 1920 and 407,907,739 pesos in 1921. Philippine trade with the United States amounted to 8,108,155 pesos in 1894, 42,343,688 pesos in 1909, 86,220,558 pesos in 1913, 395,012,081 pesos in 1920 and 248,973,616 pesos in 1921. Expressed in percentages, Philippine-American trade represented 13 per cent of the total foreign trade of the Philippines in 1894, 32 per cent in 1909, 43 per cent in 1913, 66 per cent in 1920 and 61 per cent in 1921. In a report on colonial tariff policies issued in 1921, the United States Tariff Commission said:

"If the colonies of other powers be divided into three groups—the open-door colonies, the British Dominions, and the dependent colonies enforcing discriminatory duties—it can be seen at once that the trade of the United States with either of the first two groups greatly exceeds that with its own colonies. The possibility of the growth of this trade is also much greater, for American merchants already have most of the trade of Porto Rico and the Philippine Islands, so that the American trade with them can grow only as the total trade of these islands continue to develop. . . ." [1]

The history of the adventures of the cotton schedule of the Philippine tariff on imports acquires significance when the figures for the principal Philippine imports are examined. In the ten-year period, 1909-1918, cotton and its manufactures were the most important imports, representing on the average 22.6 per cent of the imports, while iron and steel and their manufactures, which came next, amounted to 11 per cent, rice, meat products and wheat flour following next in order of importance respectively.[2]

These changes in the countries of origin of the imports into the Philippines as well as in the countries of destination of her exports presumably were effected mainly by the tariff legislation governing the trade relations between the Philippines and the United States. It is difficult to imagine other causes, non-existent before the Spanish-American war but operating with such force after that conflict, which would account for the very material changes which have been described in the distribution of the foreign trade of the Philippine Islands.

[1] U. S. Tariff Commission, *Itroductory Survey of Colonial Tariff Policies* (1921), p. 23. The figures for the foreign trade of the Philippines are found in *Statistical Bulletin*, nos. 2, 3 and 4 issued by the Bureau of Commerce and Industry of the Philippine Islands.

[2] Computed from table no. 46, *Bulletin*, no. 2, Bureau of Commerce and Industry, Philippine Islands.

A parallel development, though not quite so pronounced, has occurred in the nationality of the vessels engaged in transporting the foreign commerce of the country. In 1909 American ships carried 4,253,226 pesos worth of merchandise out of a total trade of 132,017,512 pesos; in 1913 the figures were 16,885,830 pesos and 202,171,484 pesos, respectively; while in 1919 American ships transported 148,842,663 pesos worth of goods out of a total foreign trade of 463,513,756 pesos. The growth in the value of Philippine-American trade was appreciated in the declaration by Senator Jones of Washington, while defending the Philippine section of the Merchant Marine Act of 1920, that he regarded that provision as one of the most important sections of the Act.

In connection with the Tariff Act of March 8, 1902, it will be remembered that the export duties on Philippine products, which were not abolished until 1913, were refunded when those products were exported for use and consumption in the United States. The same law provided for the turning over into the Philippine treasury of the customs duties collected on Philippine products entering the United States. This provision remained in force until the establishment of qualified free trade in 1909. The refundable export duties collected in the period, 1906-1912, amounted to 4,595,625 pesos, while the import duties which the United States refunded to the Philippine treasury in the same period reached a figure only slightly higher, being 4,999,502 pesos in amount.[1]

There is not much to be said in connection with the results of the legislation on the public debt, franchises, and the currency. On May 31, 1922 Congress extended the limit of bonded indebtedness of the Islands to 10 per cent

[1] These figures were supplied to the writer by the Bureau of Insular Affairs of the War Department.

of the assessed valuation of their property, which meant a debt limit in the neighborhood of $75,000,000. Issues of Philippine government bonds already made in the United States cover practically the entire amount. A great portion of the proceeds of the new bond issues was made necessary by the new currency legislation in 1922, which increased the size of the Gold Standard Fund and the Treasury Certificates Reserve Fund in order to guarantee the sale of exchange between New York and Manila and thus maintain the parity of the Philippine silver peso with gold.

The severe restrictions imposed by the Act of Congress of July 1, 1902 on the sale of public lands have been one important cause of the fact that but a very small portion of the public domain has been disposed of by sale or given away as homesteads. From 1904 to 1918 only 26,001 homestead entries had been allowed involving an area of 339,481 hectares or 838,702 acres. Applications for the sale of public land to the number of 744 had been approved and 24,298 hectares of 60,745 acres sold.[1] The Philippine legislature increased the allotment for homesteads in 1919 by half, making each homestead 24 hectares (60 acres) instead of 16 hectares (40 acres).[2] These limitations have probably been mainly responsible for the absence of any vigorous attempts on the part of foreign capital to develop agricultural plantations in the Islands worked by native labor but under foreign ownership and management. In this respect the experience of the Philippines has been very different from that of other tropical colonies. There has not taken place any rapid agricultural development through the importation of foreign capital. However, with the growth of Philippine autonomy the dangers attendant upon

[1] Table no. 97, of *Statistical Bulletin*, no. 3. *op. cit.*

[2] See Act no. 2874 of the Philippine Legislature, approved November 29, 1919.

the liberalizing of the public land laws are very materially lessened. Indeed, the burden of complaint on the part of those who would hasten the economic development of the country has been the failure to attract foreign capital. That the charge is not entirely without foundation is shown by the annual report of the Governor-General for the year 1919 giving an estimate of the amount of foreign capital invested in the Philippines.[1] The investments, by countries, were:

Great Britain	968,609,682 pesos
United States	553,022,200 pesos
Germany	174,486,264 pesos (most of the property was seized during the war)
Japan	131,500,000 pesos
Netherlands	23,919,000 pesos

Whether or not these policies, the legislative histories of which have been examined and the results so summarily outlined, were or are justified does not concern us here.

These results stated, the question arises: What has been the underlying concept in the mind of the American Congress in these various acts of legislation? It may be laid down as an unquestioned fact that America's Philippine policy has shown a liberality unequalled in the history of other colonial Powers. Yet that can not be a sufficient answer to the query. If, instead of the American Congress, it had been a Filipino legislature which took charge of legislation, would the results have been the same? And, what is even more important, would the same arguments prove as decisive in the one case as in the other? For, to the Filipino, the issue is not so much the contrast between the absence of gross evils in America's rule as compared with the rather black picture painted by the older colonial

[1] P. 10.

Powers, but rather this: Has America taken care of Philippine interests as she would of her own?

From an *a priori* judgment, and considering the mechanics of a democratic government, only a negative answer is possible. However fondly we may hope for that political millenium, wherein politicians will truly become their neighbor's keeper, the fact is unescapable that a legislator's pious aspirations, like a new year's resolution, need for their realization a positive sanction, namely, either the prospect of involuntary retirement from the arena of public life, or the enjoyment of popular acclaim. It is not a difficult feat of the imagination to conceive of situations in which the average legislator may discern a conflict between Philippine and American interests, taken separately or in the aggregate.

But whether or not one believes completely in the theory that the relationship between the care of political fences and those finished products of the popular will known as statutes is one of cause and effect, a dispassionate analysis of the place which the Philippine problem occupies in American politics will similarly lead to a negative answer.

The American government is a government of public opinion. On questions that are simple and of tremendous import, easily comprehensible and vital to their daily lives, the American people speaks in such tones of emphasis as no American legislature would dare disregard. But the Philippine problem does not have enough of the simplicity and has not sufficiently assumed, after the campaign of 1900, the aspects of a paramount issue to command the attention and enlist the serious interest of the vast majority of the American people. If, on the one hand, distance, which is so powerful an ally of sentiment, operates here as an attraction for the romanticist, on the other, the threads of commerce woven during the last two decades furnish a powerful appeal to the realist. Thus these two portions of the public which acquire an interest in Philppine affairs neutralize each other, and between them lies the overwhelming majority of the people, uninformed and uninterested.

Superimposed on this limted interest, is the difficulty of acquirng and assimilating facts about a country ten thousand miles away. Even if non-partisan statistical tables are obtained, the necessity of securing a proper perspective and appreciating national interests and idiosyncrasies are obstacles that only the incurable optimist would minimize.

And, assuming the necessary interest to have been stimulated and accurate information disseminated, there would still remain the danger of the Philippines losing not through the "collusion" but because of the "collision" between opposing *blocs*.

Illustrative of these different theoretical propositions that have been advanced is the story of the Congressional mind on economic legislation for the Philippines. While there was a strong and sincere desire to regard the welfare of the islands as a sacred trust, still the interests of the United States were always the decisive factors.[1] In cases where those interests were found to be in accord with Philippine interests, the result has been speedy legislation. In other cases where the possibility of injury to America appeared, there has been hesitation and delay. This is so because, as was stated by Senator Lodge, the cardinal principle of American statesmanship is the care of American interests.

[1] Professor Willis expressed this in much stronger language when, writing in 1905, he said: "On the whole, it must be concluded that in economic matters Congress has pursued toward the Philippines a policy of slavish subservience to special American interests. . . ." *Our Philippine Problem*, p. 311; see also Chamberlin, *The Philippine Problem*. For a criticism of Professor Willis's book, see Leroy in *Political Science Quarterly*, vol. xxi, no. 2.

BIBLIOGRAPHY

A. Reports and Documents

Bureau of Commerce and Industry (Philippine Islands), *Statistical Bulletin*, nos. 2, 3 and 4.

Conant, C. A., *Special Report to the Secretary of War on Coinage and Banking in the Philippine Islands*, Washington, 1901.

Commission on International Exchange, *Report* on the introduction of the gold-exchange standard into China and other silver-using countries, published as *H. Doc.* 144, 58th Cong., 2nd Sess.

Congressional Record:

55th Congress, 3rd Session.
56th Congress, 1st Session.
56th Congress, 2nd Session.
57th Congress, 1st Session.
57th Congress, 2nd Session.
58th Congress, 2nd Session.
58th Congress, 3rd Session.
59th Congress, 1st Session.
60th Congress, 1st Session.
61st Congress, 1st Session.
63rd Congress, 1st Session.
66th Congress, 1st Session.
66th Congress, 2nd Session.
67th Congress, 1st Session.
67th Congress, 2nd Session.

Customs Tariff and Regulations for the Philippine Islands, Gov't Printing Office, Washington, 1899.

Democratic *Campaign Textbook*, 1912.

Edwards, C. R., *Memorandum on Currency and Exchange in the Philippine Islands*, Washington, 1900.

Harden, E. M., *Report on Financial and Industrial Conditions in the Philippine Islands*, Washington, 1898.

Hearings on the Philippine Tariff, House Committee on Ways and Means, 58th Cong., 3rd Sess.

Hearings on the Philippine Tariff, House Committee on Ways and Means, 59th Congress, 1st Session.

Hearings on the Tariff, Bureau of Public Printing, Manila, 1905.

Hearings on the bill to increase the limit of bonded indebtedness of the Philippines, Committee on Insular Affairs, May, 1921.

Hearings on the bill further to increase the limit of bonded indebtedness of the Philippines, Committee on Insular Affairs, February-March, 1922.

House Documents:

No. 14, on the proposed tariff revision law of 1909 for the Philippines, 61st Cong., 1st Sess.

No. 1071, on the sale of the friar lands in the Philippines, 61st Cong., 3rd Sess.

No. 1326, on the sale of the friar lands, 61st Cong., 3rd Sess.

House Reports:

No. 2496, on the Civil Government Law of 1902, 57th Cong., 1st Sess.

No. 2907, on the bill (December 5, 1902) to reduce tariff rates on Philippine products.

No. 1904, on S. bill (2259) to regulate shipping in trade between America and the Philippines, 58th Cong., 2nd Sess.

No. 4600, on the bill (January 23, 1905) to amend the tariff of the Philippines, 58th Cong., 3rd Sess.

No. 20, on the H. bill (December 4, 1905) to reduce the tariff rates on Philippine products, 59th Cong., 1st Sess.

No. 582, on the bill (January 25, 1906) to amend the tariff laws of the Philippines, 59th Cong., 1st Sess.

No. 3214, on the Coastwise Shipping Act of April 30, 1906. 59th Cong., 1st Sess.

No. 7, on the Law of August 5, 1909 to amend the tariff laws of the Philippines, 61st Cong., 1st Sess.

No. 2289, on the administration of the friar lands in the Philippines, 61st Cong., 3rd Sess.

No. 443, on the Merchant Marine Act of June 5, 1920, 66th Cong., 1st Sess.

No. 55, on H. bill 5756 to increase the limit of bonded indebtedness, 67th Cong., 1st Sess.

No. 874, on H. bill 10442 further increasing the debt limit, 67th Cong., 2nd Sess.

No. 3023 and 3834, on the Coinage Law of 1903, 57th Cong., 2nd Sess.

The Insular Cases, Gov't Printing Office, Washington, 1901.

Jenks, J. W., *Report on Certain Economic Questions in the English and Dutch Colonies in the Orient to the Secretary of War*, Washington, 1902.

Messages and Papers of the Presidents, vol. xv.

Official Gazette of the Philippine Islands, 1904-1921.

Philippine Reports, vol. xv.

Papers relating to Foreign Relations, etc., 1898.

Report, Navy Department, 1898.
Reports, Philippine Commission, 1900-1916.
Reports, Bureau of Insular Affairs, 1902-1922.
Reports, Secretary of War, 1900-1922.
Republican *Campaign Textbook*, 1900, 1904, 1908.
Senate Documents:
No. 62, on the Treaty of Paris, 55th Cong., 3rd Sess.
No. 171, on the correspondence relating to the Philippine customs tariff of 1901, 57th Cong., 1st Sess.
No. 134, on certain memoranda relating to tariff between the United States and the Philippines (1902), 57th Cong., 1st Sess.
No. 182, on the Treaty of Paris and the McEnery Resolution (S. J. Res. 240, 55th Cong., 3rd Sess.), 57th Cong., 1st Sess.
No. 331, Hearings before the Senate Committee on the Philippines in relation to affairs in the Philippines, 57th Cong., 1st Sess.
No. 124, Hearings on Coastwise Shipping Legislation, 58th Cong., 2nd Sess.
Senate Reports:
No. 915, on the Civil Government Law of 1902, 57th Cong., 1st Sess.
No. 2586, on H. bill 15702 (December 5, 1902) to reduce tariff rates on Philippine products, 57th Cong., 2nd Sess.
No. 137, on S. bill 2259 to regulate shipping in trade between the United States and the Philippines, 58th Cong., 2nd Sess.
No. 573, on the Merchant Marine Act of June 5, 1920, 66th Cong., 2nd Sess.
No. 181, on H. bill 5756 to increase the limit of bonded indebtedness, 67th Cong., 1st Sess.
No. 718, on H. bill 10442 further increasing the debt limit, 67th Cong., 2nd Sess.
U. S. Reports, vols. 182, 183, 195.
U. S. Statutes, vols. 31-36, 38-39, 41.
U. S. Tariff Commission, *Introductory Survey of Colonial Tariff Policies*, Washington, 1921.

B. Newspapers and Magazines

Annals of the American Academy of Political and Social Science, Nov., 1902.
Columbia Law Review, Nov., 1901.
Journal of Political Economy, March, 1903.
Philippines Herald, Manila, Jan., 1923.
New York Times, 1898-1899.
New York Daily Tribune, 1900.
North American Review, Aug., 1901.
Political Science Quarterly, vol. xvi.
Yale Review, Aug., 1901.

C. Secondary Material and Other References

Beard, C. A., *Contemporary American History*, New York, 1914.

Blount, J. H., *The American Occupation of the Philippines*, New York, 1912.

Chamberlin, F. C., *The Philippine Problem*, Boston, 1913.

Elliot, C. B., *The Philippines to the End of the Military Regime*, Indianapolis, 1916.

——, *The Philippines to the End of the Commission Government*, Indianapolis, 1916.

Harrison, F. B., *The Corner-Stone of Philippine Independence*, New York, 1922.

Hoar, G. F., *Autobiography of Seventy Years*, New York, 1903.

Kemmerer, E. W., *Modern Currency Reforms*, New York, 1916.

Latané, J. H., *America as a World Power*, New York, 1907.

Le Roy, J. A., *The Americans in the Philippines*, Boston and New York, 1914.

Malcolm, G., *Government of the Philippine Islands*, Rochester, New York, 1916.

Olcott, C. S., *Life of William McKinley*, New York and Boston, 1916.

Thayer, W. R., *Life and Letters of John Hay*, Boston, 1915.

Willis, H. P., *Our Philippine Problem*, New York, 1905.

Worcester, D. C., *The Philippines Past and Present*, New York, 1913.

INDEX

Bei Fragen zur Produktsicherheit wenden Sie sich bitte an:
If you have any questions regarding product safety,
please contact:

Walter de Gruyter GmbH
Genthiner Straße 13
10785 Berlin
productsafety@degruyterbrill.com